FTCE

Elementary Education K-6 Practice Questions

Mometrix

TEST PREPARATION

Dear Future Exam Success Story

First of all, **THANK YOU** for purchasing Mometrix study materials!

Second, congratulations! You are one of the few determined test-takers who are committed to doing whatever it takes to excel on your exam. **You have come to the right place.** We developed these practice tests with one goal in mind: to deliver you the best possible approximation of the questions you will see on test day.

Standardized testing is one of the biggest obstacles on your road to success, which only increases the importance of doing well in the high-pressure, high-stakes environment of test day. Your results on this test could have a significant impact on your future, and these practice tests will give you the repetitions you need to build your familiarity and confidence with the test content and format to help you achieve your full potential on test day.

Your success is our success

We would love to hear from you! If you would like to share the story of your exam success or if you have any questions or comments in regard to our products, please contact us at **800-673-8175** or **support@mometrix.com**.

Thanks again for your business and we wish you continued success!

Sincerely,
The Mometrix Test Preparation Team

TABLE OF CONTENTS

Practice Test #1

Language Arts and Reading

1. Among digital networking's educational advantages, which most transforms social interactions?

a. Linking digitally saved resources to one another
b. Embedded links to references and learning supports
c. Virtually instant access to global communications
d. Diverse formats more similar to diverse learners

2. Which of the following methods would give students the most *objective* feedback to enable them to monitor their own performance and progress in speaking and enacting through giving oral reports and presentations?

a. Having classmates offer peer reviews
b. Having a teacher evaluate their work
c. Comparing their work to classmates' work
d. Viewing videos of their performance

Refer to the following for question 3:

> In preparation for writing a paper, a class has been instructed to skim a number of internet and print documents.

3. The students are being asked to:

a. Read the documents several times, skimming to a deeper level of understanding each time.
b. Read the documents quickly, looking for those that offer the most basic, general information.
c. Read the documents quickly, looking for key words in order to gather the basic premise of each.
d. Read the documents carefully, looking for those that offer the most in-depth information.

4. For making speeches, which nonverbal behaviors enhance audience perceptions of speaker credibility?

a. Making eye contact with certain listeners
b. Making random/unrelated body motions
c. Making startling/novel facial expressions
d. Making gestures congruent with meaning

5. Which type of nonverbal message deals with belonging, control, respect, or disapproval?

a. Emotive messages
b. Relational messages
c. Relationship messages
d. Interpersonal messages

6. Commercials for a mobile service provider frequently reiterate the question, "Can you hear me now?" Which technique of persuasion does this best represent?

a. Pathos
b. Slogan use
c. Bandwagon
d. Testimonial

7. An advertisement for a prescription eye drop features a woman identified as a doctor, who both recommends the product to a patient, and she also says she uses it herself with good results. This involves which method(s) of appeal?

a. Expert opinion
b. Testimonial
c. Bandwagon
d. (a) and (b)

8. A teacher designs lessons for the upcoming week. During the first part of the week, the teacher is going to divide the class into two sections. While one group is working independently on their projects, the other group will sit in a circle. The teacher has broken a story up into several sections, and each student will read a section aloud. The teacher will note for her records how many errors a student makes. She will also administer a brief verbal "quiz" to which the students will respond in writing. The combination of verbal reading results and comprehension quiz results will give her a better understanding of each child's abilities and/or needs. What kind of assessment did this teacher use?

a. Cloze-style
b. Informal reading inventory
c. Student response form
d. Articulation assessment

9. Third-grade students typically receive their spelling word lists each Monday so that they can practice them at home before the test on Friday. While their teacher is pleased that the students usually receive high grades on spelling tests, she observes that they misspell those same words when writing in journals or doing classwork. How should this teacher modify her instruction?

a. Post a list of vocabulary words when the students are writing to help them recall correct spellings.
b. Integrate spelling words into writing, reading, grammar, phonics, and other activities to help students learn the words in a variety of contexts.
c. Provide more time, such as a two-week period, between tests so that students have more time to study.
d. Review the words before certain activities to increase immediate recall of correct spellings.

10. Which of these most accurately represents a characteristic of the Language Experience Approach (LEA) to literacy instruction?

a. Children get to interact with published text in books.
b. Children get to use their own experiences and words.
c. Children get to write down the stories they compose.
d. Children get to read text in books aloud to a teacher.

11. To help students select the content and format they will use in writing, what should teachers include in their instruction?

a. They should have students consider swaying reader opinions more than giving proof.
b. They should have students consider what readers will agree with instead of disagree with.
c. They should have students consider not what to impart, but what their readers know.
d. They should have students consider what information their readers share in common with them.

12. What approach would be most appropriate for teachers to solicit reflective responses from students about how their ELA curriculum and assessments are designed and used?

a. Having students take questionnaires
b. Having students write in journals
c. Having students rate teachers
d. Having students write essays

13. Teachers must consider student developmental levels when assigning cooperative learning projects and/or discussions. For example, students are bored by topics at younger age levels and lost by topics at older ones. In addition to chronological age, which other developmental level does this example relate to most?

a. Social developmental levels
b. Cognitive developmental levels
c. Emotional developmental levels
d. Behavioral developmental levels

14. How can Lexile measures best help teachers and students choose texts to fit student abilities and interests?

a. By identifying the grade levels of many books and articles
b. By finding only texts exactly matching a student's number
c. By identifying text and student reading levels via numbers
d. By assigning a number to every book and article published

15. Which of these is more characteristic of a summative assessment?

a. The teacher administers it frequently during instruction.
b. The teacher uses its results to inform teaching changes.
c. The teacher gives it after lessons, units, or school years are complete.
d. The teacher relies on it for individualizing student data.

16. Mr. Harris divides his 3rd-grade English class into two sections each day. Approximately 60% of the class period is spent on phonics and sight word practice, and 40% is spent on learning comprehension strategies. Which statement is most true regarding Mr. Harris' approach?

a. This approach neglects several important components of language instruction.
b. This approach will bore the students and possibly create negative feelings about English class.
c. This approach will provide the best balance of reading instruction for this age group.
d. This approach could be improved by spending equal amounts of time on each component, as they are equally important.

17. Collaborative Strategic Reading (CSR) is a teaching technique that depends on two teaching practices. These practices are:

a. Cooperative learning and reading comprehension
b. Cooperative reading and metacognition
c. Reading comprehension and metacognition
d. Cooperative learning and metacognition

18. Which of these sets of factors would most greatly affect a student's reading comprehension in class and on tests?

a. Oral language development, written language development and eating a healthy breakfast.
b. Word analysis skills, sight word knowledge and ability to monitor understanding.
c. Vocabulary development, sight word knowledge and reference skills.
d. Prior knowledge, good classroom participation and academic performance in other subjects.

19. A fluent reader does NOT:

a. Consistently read at a sufficient rate of speed
b. Pause frequently to sound out difficult words
c. Adjust pitch to reflect punctuation
d. Recognize words rapidly and automatically

20. Which of the following is true about how teachers can cultivate print awareness in young children?

a. It is effective to have children narrate picture books and give them matching reinforcements.
b. It is superfluous to use large-print texts for reading to younger children who cannot read yet.
c. Teachers should label things/areas in classrooms using either pictures or words, but not both.
d. When reading storybooks to young children, the texts should use novel, unpredictable words.

21. Early in the school year, all members of a group of kindergarten students are able to chant the alphabet. The teacher is now teaching the students what the alphabet looks like in written form. The teacher points to a letter, and the students vocalize the corresponding sound. Alternatively, the teacher vocalizes a phoneme and a student points to it on the alphabet chart. The teacher is using ____________ in her instruction.

a. letter–sound correspondence
b. rote memorization
c. predictive analysis
d. segmentation

22. Which of the following strategies would not be helpful in building the word-identification skills of emergent readers?

a. Allowing for invented spelling in written assignments or in-class work.
b. Reinforcing phonemic awareness while reading aloud.
c. Using dictionaries to look up unfamiliar words.
d. Studying and reviewing commonly used sight words at the students' ability level.

23. Which of the following phonological awareness activities is easiest for children?

a. Naming rhyming words for a word
b. Picking rhyming words from lists
c. Recognizing words that rhyme
d. These are all equally difficult.

24. Which of the following is true regarding children's reading fluency?

a. The lack of reading fluency is always due to word-decoding deficits.
b. Children's motivation to read is unaffected by their reading fluency.
c. Some children need only more reading practice to develop fluency.
d. Fluency has equal impact on school performance at all grade levels.

25. Which of the following instructional strategies would likely help students the most in understanding the difference between denotation and connotation and help them learn to identify the connotation of a word in context?

a. Providing example sentences in multiple choice questions asking for a word's connotation
b. Filling out a Venn diagram with sets of words that have connotations, denotations, or both
c. Assigning a reading where students identify and highlight words that have connotations
d. Giving word definitions and asking students to describe the feelings elicited by each definition

26. Suppose a teacher is helping students categorize animals as carnivores, herbivores, and omnivores using an explanation in a biology text. Which of the following types of exercises will be of most help to students in identifying these categories and their definitions as explained in the text?

a. Summarizing
b. Cloze sentences
c. Creative extension
d. Term memorization

27. Which statement accurately reflects a principle regarding self-questioning techniques for increasing student reading comprehension?

a. Asking only what kinds of "expert questions" fit the text's subject matter
b. Asking only those questions that the text raises for the individual student
c. Asking how each text portion relates to chapter main ideas is unnecessary
d. Asking how the text information fits with what the student already knows

28. An understanding of the meanings of prefixes and suffixes such as *dis, mis, un, re, able,* and *ment* is important primarily for:

a. Reading comprehension
b. Word recognition
c. Vocabulary building
d. Reading fluency

29. When teaching students relationships between sounds and letters and between letters and words, what practices should teachers best follow?

a. Use a variety of instructional techniques, but including only the auditory and visual modes.
b. Incorporate multisensory modalities within a variety of instructional strategies and materials.
c. Always adhere to the same exact instructional method and materials to ensure consistency.
d. Introduce similar-looking letters and similar-sounding phonemes together for discrimination.

30. Which of these statements about guided reading is NOT true?

a. Guided reading promotes fluency.
b. Guided reading fosters social interaction.
c. Flexible grouping allows students to progress at their own rates.
d. Guided reading is generally a whole-class activity.

31. Which of the following reading strategies is LEAST likely to be effective in supporting active reading for students before they read?

a. Guessing what will happen
b. Drawing a story map of predictions
c. Summarizing current knowledge of the topic
d. Identifying questions that the text may answer

32. According to a large body of research, how is systematic phonics instruction most effective?

a. For the majority of K-6 students, with the exception of students having difficulty with learning to read
b. When it is provided to K–6 students as an instructional program separate from any reading instruction.
c. With pre-K–2 students but not older, and paired with phonemic awareness but not other instruction
d. In the context of comprehensive reading programs including fluency, vocabulary, and comprehension

33. Which of the following choices represents the smallest unit of language that possesses semantic meaning?

a. Morpheme
b. Grapheme
c. Phoneme
d. Word stem

34. A teacher asks her students to say the word *map*. She then says, "Change the /m/ sound to a /t/ sound. What word do you have now?" Which phonemic awareness skill are students practicing?

a. Alliteration
b. Segmenting
c. Blending onset and rime
d. Phoneme substitution

35. Which of the following most accurately defines information literacy?

a. The set of skills required for reading and comprehending information
b. The set of skills necessary to amass a comprehensive base of knowledge
c. The set of skills required for the finding, retrieval, analysis, and use of information
d. The set of skills necessary for effectively communicating information to others

36. In selecting literature for children, the most important first step a teacher should perform is to evaluate

a. Whether the characters are interesting
b. Whether the plots are appealing
c. Class composition and preferences
d. The reading level of the material

37. Which type of poetic form is characterized by three lines in free verse that contain a total of 17 syllables, with each line frequently having five, seven, and five syllables, respectively?

a. Haiku
b. Sonnet
c. Limerick
d. Cinquain

38. To select materials for partner reading, which of the following should the teacher do?

a. Identify materials that are suitable for the higher reader's instructional reading level
b. Have each student partner in a pair read a different passage from the same material
c. Select enough materials for every pair of students to read two new passages a week
d. Identify materials that are suitable for the lower reader's independent reading level

39. Which statement about the relationship between conflict and plot is most accurate?

a. Conflict is what drives the plot of a story forward.
b. Resolving the main conflict is often not the protagonist's primary endeavor.
c. Emotional, mental, and moral conflicts impact plot less than physical conflicts do.
d. The climax of a plot only occurs after the main conflict has been resolved.

40. In which genre does the literature rely on the reader's suspension of disbelief about magical and mythical creatures?

a. Science fiction
b. Fantasy
c. Action and adventure
d. Historical fiction

41. Which of these statements is true of informational text comprehension?

a. It relies entirely on retrieving important information.
b. It depends on the reader's indirect reasoning ability alone.
c. It requires the reader to recall information and make inferences.
d. It includes inferences made by the reader but not their prior knowledge.

42. Which of the following literary elements are most likely to be found in both fictional narratives and nonfictional informational text?

a. The writing style of the author
b. Labeled diagrams and photos
c. Excitement and drama
d. Themes and plots

43. Which of the following processes used in writing is the most complex?

a. Evaluation
b. Application
c. Comprehension
d. Knowledge recall

44. If a teacher assigns students to pairs for cooperative writing partnerships, which of the following should their activities include?

a. One student should write, and the other should review the work.
b. Each partner in a pair takes turns being the writer and the reviewer.
c. Each student should provide only positive feedback to the other.
d. Each student should give only constructive feedback to the other.

45. When teachers assign students to small groups for collaborative writing, which of these applies?

a. Teachers should only set individual performance expectations for individual, not group work.
b. Teachers should expect student groups to self-manage, and not interfere by giving structure.
c. Classmates in collaborative groups should give each other positive feedback, not corrections.
d. Classmates in collaborative groups should give each other constructive and positive feedback.

46. Among these procedural devices that help students plan and revise writing, which is helpful as an aid for remembering key sets of information?

a. Outlines
b. Checklists
c. Mnemonic devices
d. Graphic organizers

47. Which of the following can the writer determine without considering the audience?

a. Purpose
b. Structure
c. Word choice
d. Amount of research

48. The main difference between a topic outline and a sentence outline is

a. a topic outline helps arrange ideas.
b. ideas are numbered or lettered in a sentence outline.
c. ideas are fully stated in a sentence outline.
d. a sentence outline only uses brief phrases or single words.

49. Students should learn to write for a variety of audiences because:

a. Writing everything just for the teacher is boring.
b. Their classmates are also a potential audience.
c. Students are more involved in their writing if the audience varies.
d. Students can make political statements with letters to the editor.

50. Among the following major types of conflicts typically included in literary plots, which one is classified as an internal conflict?

a. Man against man
b. Man against nature
c. Man against society
d. Man against himself

Social Science

51. A country's currency increases in value on foreign currency exchange markets. What will happen as a result?

I. Exports will drop
II. Imports will rise
III. The balance of payments will rise

a. I only
b. II only
c. I and II
d. II and III

52. According to Karl Marx, which two groups are in continual conflict?

a. Farmers and landowners
b. Workers and owners
c. Kings and nobles
d. Politicians and voters

53. Which statement about factors related to the growth of the US economy between 1945 and 1970 is NOT correct?

a. The Baby Boom's greatly increased birth rates contributed to economic growth during this time.
b. The reduction in military spending after World War II contributed to the stronger US economy.
c. Government programs and growing affluence nearly quadrupled college enrollments in 20 years.
d. Increased mobility and bigger families caused fast suburban expansion, especially in the Sunbelt.

54. An action's opportunity cost is best explained in terms of which of the following?

a. The minimum amount a business must borrow for the action
b. The opportunities given up in order to pursue that action
c. The percentage of one's overall budget that the action requires
d. The cost of a long-term action adjusted for inflation

55. Which of the following is NOT a direct input in the basic economic concept of a country's gross domestic product (GDP)?

a. The size of its workforce
b. The amount of its capital
c. Technology in place
d. Education of its workforce

56. Which of the following is most likely to benefit from inflation?

a. A bond investor who owns fixed-rate bonds
b. A retired widow with no income other than fixed Social Security payments
c. A person who has taken out a fixed-rate loan
d. A local bank who has loaned money out at fixed rate

57. John Maynard Keynes advocated what?

a. Supply-side economics
b. Demand-side economics
c. Laissez faire economics
d. The Laffer Curve

58. Economics is best defined as the study of what?

a. Scarcity
b. Business
c. Trade
d. Supply and demand

Refer to the following for question 59:

A first-grade teacher is planning a geography unit focused on how the weather impacts the way that people live. This unit will focus on how weather differs in the regions near the poles, the tropical regions, and the mid-latitudes.

59. What should the teacher tell students that the main reason that tropical regions near the Equator tend to experience relatively constant year-round temperatures is?

a. They are usually located near the ocean.
b. The angle at which sunlight hits them remains relatively constant throughout the year.
c. They are located along the "Ring of Fire."
d. They do not have seasons.

Refer to the following for question 60:

US Census Data

(All population figures are per 200,000 square miles of land area)

Date	Northeastern US Rural Areas	Northeastern US Urban Areas
1890	Population average of around 7.5 million	Population average of around 12.5 million
1930	Population average of around 11 million	Population average of around 30 million

60. Which of the following inferences is best supported by this US Census Data chart?

a. Rural to urban migration was a probable trend between the years 1890 and 1930.
b. Urban to rural migration was a probable pattern between the years 1890 and 1930.
c. Urban areas grew in population numbers, but rural areas had a decreased population between 1890 and 1930.
d. Rural areas grew in population numbers, but urban areas had a decreased population between 1890 and 1930.

61. Which soil horizon consists of weathered rock?

a. A horizon
b. C horizon
c. O horizon
d. R horizon

62. As used in geographical maps, which of the following is a synonym for the term *latitude?*

a. Longitude
b. Parallel
c. Meridian
d. Coordinate

63. Which state covers the most area?

a. New York
b. Texas
c. California
d. Alaska

64. The physical geography of a region most directly affects which of the following?

a. The religious beliefs of the native population
b. The family structure of the native population
c. The dietary preferences of the native population
d. The language spoken by the native population

65. On which of the following maps would the scale be largest?

a. A map of Benelux nations
b. A map of Senegal
c. A map of Rio de Janeiro
d. A map of Greenwich Village

66. How many intermediate directions are there?

a. 2
b. 4
c. 8
d. 16

67. One of the earliest political parties in the United States was the Federalist Party. Its decline is best explained by:

a. A failure to organize state political parties
b. The enmity of wealthy Americans
c. Its opposition to the War of 1812
d. Its advocacy of a strong central government

68. Which of the following examples is protected as an expression of free speech?

a. Draftees of the Vietnam War who burned their draft cards
b. A radio personality who states on air that the President should be shot over his most recent budget proposal
c. Pro-life protesters who carry "wanted" signs displaying the photos and home/work addresses of abortion providers during a legally sanctioned protest
d. A high school teacher who allows her students to use profanity when creating poetry

69. Thomas Jefferson embraced a theological philosophy called deism, which promotes which of the following?

a. Abolition
b. Atheism
c. Separation of church and state
d. A theocratic central government

70. Civic responsibility differs from personal responsibility in that the subject matter of civic responsibility is mainly which of the following?

a. Fair reporting of government actions
b. Fair dealings between governments
c. A person's responsibilities as a citizen
d. A person's responsibilities as a government worker

71. "Old enough to fight, old enough to vote" became a slogan for a youth voting rights movement after the World War II military draft age was lowered to 18, while 21 remained the minimum voting age. The Vietnam War draft brought more urgency to the youth voting rights movement and resulted in which amendment to lower the voting age to 18?

a. 24th Amendment
b. 25th Amendment
c. 26th Amendment
d. 27th Amendment

72. As a form of government, what does *oligarchy* mean?

a. Rule by one
b. Rule by a few
c. Rule by law
d. Rule by many

73. How long can members of the Federal Judiciary serve?

a. Four years
b. Eight years
c. For life
d. Six years

74. The concept of checks and balances is evident in which of the following?

a. Federal judiciary appeals
b. Presidential veto
c. States' rights
d. The House and the Senate

75. Which statement describes the authority of most local officials?

a. Members of local government are generally elected by the people, but their authority is granted by the state.
b. Members of local government are given their authority directly from the people.
c. Members of local government have constitutionally-granted authority.
d. Members of local government are elected by the people, but the state Supreme Court determines their authority.

76. What would be the best title for this list that summarizes what all of the items on the list have in common?

- Communist North Korea invaded South Korea in 1950.
- President Truman worried that the Soviet Union and China planned to expand communism throughout Asia.
- The United Nations passed a resolution in 1950 urging United Nations member countries to give assistance to South Korea in their battle against North Korea.

a. Reasons Why the Policy of Containment was Ineffective
b. Reasons for United States Involvement in the Korean War
c. Reasons for the Popularity of McCarthyism in the United States
d. Reasons Why the House Un-American Activities Committee Formed

77. Which of the following statements is NOT true regarding English expansionism in the 16th century?

a. England's defeat of the Spanish Armada in 1588 brought a decisive end to their war with Spain.
b. King Henry VIII's desire to divorce Catherine of Aragon strengthened English expansionism.
c. Queen Elizabeth's support for the Protestant Reformation strengthened English expansionism.
d. Sir Francis Drake and other English sea captains plundered the goods that the Spaniards took from indigenous peoples.

78. Which Founding Father was governor of Connecticut during and after the Revolutionary War, and was the only governor of a British colony who sided with colonists during the Revolutionary War?

a. Charles Carroll
b. Benjamin Rush
c. Jonathan Trumbull
d. John Witherspoon

79. Put the following events in order from oldest to most recent.

1) Martin Luther King led the March on Washington.
2) Brown v. Board of Education overturned the policy of "separate but equal" education.
3) The Student Non-Violent Coordinating Committee began staging sit-ins at segregated lunch counters in the South.
4) The arrest of Rosa Parks sparked the Montgomery Bus Boycott.

a. 2,4,3,1
b. 1,3,2,4
c. 3,4,1,2
d. 2,1,4,3

80. The telephone was a solution to which of the following problems with the telegraph?

a. Telegraph lines were thick and difficult to maintain.
b. Telegraph messages could only be received by people who had specialized equipment.
c. Telegraphs could only relay one message at a time.
d. Telegraphs frequently broke down if subject to extended use.

81. Which of the following is NOT a true statement regarding the Louisiana Purchase?

a. Jefferson sent a delegation to Paris to endeavor to purchase only the city of New Orleans from Napoleon.
b. Napoleon, anticipating US intrusions into Louisiana, offered to sell the US the entire Louisiana territory.
c. The American delegation accepted Napoleon's offer, though they were only authorized to buy New Orleans.
d. The Louisiana Purchase, once it was completed, increased the territory of the US by 50% overnight.

82. Which of the following was NOT an immediate effect of rapid urban growth in the 1800s?

a. Poor sanitation conditions in the cities
b. Epidemics of diseases in the cities
c. Inadequate police and fire protection
d. Widespread urban political corruption

83. During the decolonization of the Cold War years, which of the following events occurred chronologically latest?

a. The Eastern Bloc and Satellite states became independent from the Soviet Union.
b. Canada became totally independent from British Parliament via the Canada Act.
c. The Bahamas, in the Caribbean, became independent from the United Kingdom.
d. The Algerian War ended, and Algeria became independent from France.

84. Which of the following statements is false regarding the Puritans?

a. In terms of their theology, the Puritans were considered Calvinists.
b. Many Puritans agreed with radical views that criticized the Swiss Calvinists.
c. Many of those identified as Calvinists opposed the Puritans.
d. The Restoration and the Uniformity Act reunified the Puritan movement and the Church of England.

Refer to the following for question 85:

"As you know, I will soon be visiting the People's Republic of China and the Soviet Union. I go there with no illusions. We have great differences with both powers. We shall continue to have great differences. But peace depends on the ability of great powers to live together on the same planet despite their differences."

85. Which president gave this speech, as he was about to become the first US President to visit the communist People's Republic of China?

a. President John F. Kennedy
b. President Lyndon B. Johnson
c. President Richard M. Nixon
d. President Gerald R. Ford

Refer to the following for question 86:

President Woodrow Wilson's "Fourteen Points" speech in 1918 included the following lines:

XIV. A general association of nations must be formed under specific covenants for the purpose of affording mutual guarantees of political independence and territorial integrity to great and small states alike.

In regard to these essential rectifications of wrong and assertions of right we feel ourselves to be intimate partners of all the governments and peoples associated together against the Imperialists. We cannot be separated in interest or divided in purpose. We stand together until the end.

86. Based on this excerpt, what was one way that Wilson's "Fourteen Points" contrasted with his pre-war position of US neutrality?

a. In 1918, Wilson agreed with the philosophy of the imperialists.
b. By 1918, Wilson thought that each nation should form its own government.
c. In this speech, Wilson believed that each nation should be able to decide its own territories.
d. In this speech, Wilson wanted to set up a League of Nations, an international organization.

87. Which of the following laws was instrumental in spurring westward migration to the Great Plains between 1860 and 1880?

a. The Homestead Act
b. The Timber Culture Act
c. The Desert Land Act
d. All of these laws were instrumental in spurring westward migration to the Great Plains during that period.

88. You are researching the Battle of the Bulge's Malmedy Massacre. Four potential sources offer conflicting accounts of one aspect of the event. Based on the principles of historical research, which source would be considered a primary source?

a. Wikipedia
b. A newspaper article written by an analyst who synthesized the accounts of several surviving soldiers over the weeks following the massacre.
c. The account of a wounded survivor written immediately following the massacre.
d. One of your teaching colleague's lecture notes.

89. What is one reason for using a secondary source over a primary source?

a. To understand an event through a first-hand account
b. Primary sources are text-only
c. To understand an event through accounts after the fact
d. Primary sources are only visual

Refer to the following for questions 90–91:

> My name is Amorosa. I am 14 years old and I live near the Gulf Coast in South Texas. My father runs an oil refinery, and my mother is a schoolteacher. I have two brothers, named Jorge and Emil—they are 16-year-old twins! After school, when there is no soccer practice, I love to spend time in the Art classroom. I love the paints, clays, fabrics, and other materials used to create beautiful things. Next year, my family and friends will celebrate my Quinceañera, a large party in honor of my 15th birthday. There will be music, food, a Court of Honor made up of my friends, and most importantly, a beautiful dress. In my city, there are talented women who design and make ball gowns that we will wear. When I celebrate my Quinceañera, I will help the dress designer create my dress.

90. Amorosa is an example of a student

a. who writes exceptionally well for a fourteen year old girl.
b. whose family maintains their cultural customs within a different national identity.
c. who exemplifies an artistic personality type that should be encouraged just as highly as are academic interests.
d. who is very focused on interpersonal relationships.

91. How could Amorosa's teacher encourage her to use her interests to build her understanding of various cultural influences and diversity?

a. Ask Amorosa to bring in pictures of all of the events surrounding the celebration to show her classmates.
b. Encourage Amorosa to research similar customs in other cultures present in Texas (e.g., Swiss, French, Native American) and compare and contrast them.
c. Require Amorosa to speak to her class about what her family's heritage means to her and how her culture has influenced the person she has become.
d. Allow Amorosa to use her artistic skills to teach so that she can work with children of all ages and backgrounds.

92. What is a correct reason for laws and rules that can be used to help young children understand important concepts of civics?

a. Laws and rules punish rather than identify unacceptable citizen behaviors.
b. Laws and rules interfere with the ability of citizens to have responsibilities.
c. Laws and rules make society and life more predictable, orderly, and secure.
d. Laws and rules grant greater powers to persons with positions of authority.

93. Which of the following is the most effective use of technology for showing a class of students the relationship between supply and demand?

a. Asking the students to maintain a class wiki listing those and other key economic terms
b. Having students look up definitions of "supply" and "demand" in an online dictionary
c. Using presentation software to show students different supply and demand curves
d. Using spreadsheet software to track the rise and fall of demand of a given product

94. A first-grade teacher has asked students to bring in a picture of something representing their heritage to create a classroom quilt. This activity is most likely intended to begin developing students' awareness of which main theme related to social studies learning?

a. Civic competence and democratic ideals
b. Awareness of one's own and others' cultures
c. Global connections
d. Individuals, groups, and institutions

95. In Government class, students are reading about and discussing controversy around immigration and naturalization laws. Which of the following Supreme Court decisions is ideal for illustrating the United States' long history of dialogue about citizenship?

a. Dred Scott v Sandford, 1857
b. Roe v Wade, 1973
c. Miranda v Arizona, 1963
d. Marbury *v Madison, 1803*

Science

96. Which of the following is a source of renewable energy?

a. Nuclear power
b. Natural gas
c. Geothermal power
d. Crude oil

97. Which of the following terms describes an intrusion of magma injected between two layers of sedimentary rock, forcing the overlying strata upward to create a dome-like form?

a. Sill
b. Dike
c. Laccolith
d. Caldera

98. If an astronomer observing the stars detects a blue shift, what could he conclude?

a. The star is moving farther away from him.
b. The star is moving closer or toward him.
c. The star is cooling down and becoming smaller.
d. The star is heating up and becoming larger.

99. Which of the following is a source of nonrenewable energy?

a. Solar power
b. Wind power
c. Wood
d. Coal

100. Which of the following is a serious direct impact of climate change?

a. Soil erosion
b. Deforestation
c. Water pollution
d. Increase in average sea level

101. Among the three types of rock on the Earth, which one is formed out of the other two?

a. Sedimentary
b. Metamorphic
c. Igneous rock
d. All three are.

102. Tropical climate zones are characterized by:

a. Extreme temperature variations between night and day
b. Extreme temperature variations between seasons
c. Frequent rainfall
d. All of the above

103. Which of the following is NOT a factor as to why lakes don't freeze solid in winter?

a. Water has its lowest volume at zero degrees Celsius.
b. As water freezes, the ice floats due to its lower density than the surrounding water.
c. Due to hydrogen bonding, ice forms six-sided crystals that have a larger volume than six water molecules.
d. The water exposed to the cold air freezes first, forming a good insulator between the air and the water beneath it.

Refer to the following for question 104:

Many fishermen will watch the tide report for the local area and get up very early or stay out late in order to have the best fishing opportunity. One night while out late fishing, a fisherman noticed that the land temperature cooled rapidly, while the ocean water stayed relatively warm.

104. What type of wind was likely created during these conditions?

a. Sea breeze
b. Land breeze
c. Monsoon
d. Trade wind

105. Before they can be used by the body as fuel, complex carbohydrates must be converted into:

a. Glucose
b. Amino acids
c. Lipids
d. Folic acid

106. A dihybrid cross is made between the dominant genes for brown eyes (B) and blonde hair (S), and the recessive genes for blue eyes (b) and red hair (s). What fraction of offspring would have the genotype BbSs in the F2 generation?

a. $\frac{1}{16}$
b. $\frac{3}{16}$
c. $\frac{4}{16}$
d. $\frac{9}{16}$

107. A length of DNA coding for a particular protein is called a(n)

a. Allele
b. Genome
c. Gene
d. Transcript

108. Which structures on a leaf surface open to release water vapor during transpiration and close during drought?

a. Pith
b. Stomata
c. Guard cells
d. Sepals

109. Which of the following best describes how the water inside an organism affects its temperature?

a. Water increases body temperature by rapidly absorbing heat due to its low heat capacity.
b. Water keeps body temperature stable by absorbing large amounts of heat with only small changes in temperature due to its high specific heat capacity.
c. Water decreases body temperature by using heat energy to evaporate from the surface of the skin.
d. Water does not affect body temperature.

110. Which of the following animal structures is NOT paired to its correct function?

a. Muscle System – controls movement through three types of muscle tissue
b. Nervous System – controls sensory responses by carrying impulses away from and toward the cell body
c. Digestive System – breaks down food for absorption into the blood stream where it is delivered to cells for respiration
d. Circulatory System – exchanges gases with the environment by delivering oxygen to the bloodstream and releasing carbon dioxide

111. Which of the following is NOT a correct statement about plants?

a. Plants have different cell structures from animals.
b. Most plants primarily obtain energy from sunlight.
c. Plants do not produce sexually.
d. The green pigment in many plants is called chlorophyll.

112. Which of the following has a simple life cycle without a metamorphosis?

a. Frog
b. Newt
c. Grasshopper
d. Human being

113. Which of the following are required by all typical organisms in order to survive?

a. Water, cells, shelter, and space
b. Food, water, cellular growth, nurturing
c. Food, water, sunlight, and air
d. Air, shelter, space, and companionship

114. Which of the following metabolic compounds is composed of only carbon, oxygen, and hydrogen?

a. Phospholipids
b. Glycogen
c. Peptides
d. RNA

115. In general, where on the periodic table of elements are the elements with the largest atomic radii located?

a. Upper-right corner
b. Upper-left corner
c. Bottom-left corner
d. Bottom-right corner

116. Which of the following describes the difference between an anabolism reaction and a catabolism reaction?

a. Anabolism undergoes ionic reactions, while catabolism undergoes covalent reactions.
b. Anabolism undergoes condensation reactions, while catabolism undergoes hydrolysis.
c. Anabolism reactions use water, while catabolism reactions do not.
d. Anabolism reactions release glucose, while catabolism reactions release water.

117. What is the scientific definition of work?

a. The amount of energy used to accomplish a job
b. The force used to move a mass over a distance
c. The amount of energy used per unit of time
d. Energy stored in an object due to its position

118. Astronauts in orbit are sometimes considered to be "weightless." Consider the three propositions about *weightlessness* and determine which ones are true.

I. Weightlessness occurs in outer space because the force of gravity becomes negligible.
II. Weightlessness occurs when a ski jumper makes a jump.
III. Weightlessness occurs when you roll a baseball on the ground.

a. I only.
b. II only.
c. I and II.
d. I, II and III.

Refer to the following for question 119:

A chemistry experiment is performed to determine the effect of a nonvolatile solute on the boiling point of water. Three trials are performed in which 10 mg, 20 mg, and 30 mg of salt are added to 500 mL of distilled water. Each solution is heated on a hot plate, and the elevated boiling points are recorded.

119. Which of the following correctly identifies the independent and dependent variables in this experiment?

a. The independent variable is the amount of salt, and the dependent variable is the temperature at which the water boils.
b. The independent variable is the amount of water, and the dependent variable is the temperature at which the water boils.
c. The independent variable is the temperature at which the water boils, and the dependent variable is the amount of salt.
d. The independent variable is the amount of salt, and the dependent variable is the amount of water.

120. In an amusement park ride, you stand on the floor of a cylindrical ring with your back touching the wall. The ring begins to rotate, slowly at first, but then faster and faster. When the ring is rotating fast enough, the floor is removed. You do not slide down but remain pressed against the wall of the ring. Which is the best explanation for why you don't fall down?

a. The centripetal force pushes you towards the wall.
b. The centripetal force changes the direction of your motion.
c. The force of friction between the wall and your body is greater than the force of gravity.
d. The rotating ring creates a weightless environment.

121. Which of the following is NOT generally true regarding solubility?

a. Increasing temperature increases the solubility of a solid in a liquid.
b. Increasing temperature increases the solubility of a gas in a liquid.
c. Increasing the pressure has little effect on the solubility of a solid in a liquid.
d. Increasing partial pressure of a gas increases the solubility of a gas in a liquid.

122. Which of the following explains why less force is required to throw a tennis ball a certain distance than a shot put?

a. The shot put must overcome inertia.
b. The tennis ball has more potential energy.
c. The shot put has greater mass.
d. The tennis ball requires horizontal projection.

123. Adding a catalyst to a reaction will do which of the following?

a. Shift the reaction equilibrium towards the products
b. Increase the temperature of the reaction
c. Decrease the energy of activation for the reaction
d. Increase the purity of the reaction products

Refer to the following for question 124:

A science teacher wants to see if her students are following proper safety procedures in a lab setting. Her students are planning to assemble and operate a small gasoline engine.

124. Which safety concern should have the highest priority?

a. An open fuel tank could release sickening fumes.
b. Fingers could be injured if caught in the gears.
c. Spilled liquids may cause a short in the starter.
d. The exhaust fumes require adequate ventilation.

Refer to the following for question 125:

Your 9th grade biology class is about to take on its first animal dissection. You have already covered the procedure in detail during class, but you know that some of the students are still feeling nervous or even a little queasy.

125. Which of the following procedures would be INCORRECT regarding dissection?

a. The specimen should be rinsed before handling.
b. Harmful chemicals should be disposed of according to district regulations.
c. Decaying specimens are never permitted.
d. Students with open sores on their hands that cannot be covered should be excused from the dissection.

126. Which of the following types of chemicals are considered generally unsafe to store together?

I. Liquids and solids
II. Acids and bases
III. Reducing agents and oxidizing agents
IV. Metals and salts

a. I, II
b. II, III
c. III, IV
d. I, IV

127. To teach early physics concepts, an EC teacher gives students an activity of rolling balls down ramps. The teacher asks them questions like what would happen if one ramp were longer or higher; if two different sizes of ramps were used; if they started two balls rolling down a ramp at the same time, etc. Which skills in the scientific process do the children use during this activity?

a. Observation and communication
b. They use every one of these skills.
c. Skills of inference and prediction
d. Measurements and comparisons

128. When working with chemicals in a laboratory, which of the following describes the use of appropriate apparel?

a. Always wear gloves and aprons or lab coats. Wear goggles when needed.
b. Always wear goggles and aprons or lab coats. Wear gloves when needed.
c. Always wear goggles and gloves. Wear aprons or lab coats when needed.
d. Always wear aprons or lab coats. Wear gloves and goggles when needed.

129. When lighting a Bunsen burner, the flame is luminous yellow. Which of the following procedures is the correct way to properly adjust this flame?

a. Decrease the air supply.
b. Increase the air supply.
c. Decrease the gas supply.
d. Increase the gas supply.

130. Of the following, which is correct about teaching early science process skills to young children?

a. Inquiry and discovery activities appeal to young children's natural curiosity.
b. Young children will not naturally question and explore, but must be taught.
c. Teachers should focus on activities outside the self to appeal to youngsters.
d. Science activities must involve scientific subjects, not cooking, artwork, etc.

131. When young children build structures from blocks and then knock them down or take them apart, which of these science concepts are they learning?

a. Concepts of shape
b. Concepts of weight
c. Part-whole relations
d. Temporal sequences

132. Students in a fourth-grade class are working in small groups to create an electromagnet and investigate ways to make it stronger or weaker. As they work, the teacher gives them red, yellow, and green color-coded cards that they can use to indicate their level of understanding. In addition to allowing the teacher to conduct formative assessments, this strategy is beneficial in promoting students' ability to do which of the following?

a. Indicate their level of engagement
b. Monitor their pace as they work
c. Determine the accuracy of their hypotheses
d. Self-assess their own progress

133. Which of the following ethical questions regarding biotechnology would be answered and regulated by the Food and Drug Administration?

a. Should the packaging of meat products that come from cloned animals be labeled?
b. Should nitrate or sulfate fertilizers be added to oil spills to assist the decomposition of crude oil by bacteria?
c. Should parents be allowed to genetically alter an embryo by choosing its physical characteristics?
d. Should cells or components of cells be used to create industrially useful products?

134. Which of the following is NOT true concerning forming and testing hypotheses?

a. A controlled experiment should have only one independent variable.
b. A controlled experiment may have several constants.
c. A good hypothesis should take all of the available background material on the topic into consideration.
d. A good hypothesis will not be disproved by testing.

135. Which of the following was the first widespread use of X-rays?

a. Medical imaging
b. Fighting cancer
c. Security scanners
d. Discovering distant galaxies

136. Which of the following is NOT true about land reclamation?

a. Land for agricultural use may be reclaimed by draining submerged wetlands.
b. Land reclamation may destroy habitats and increase biodiversity.
c. Land reclamation creates new lands from ocean beds, riverbeds, or lakebeds.
d. Land reclamation may result in soil liquefaction during earthquakes.

137. Burning fossil fuels releases sulfur dioxide and nitrogen dioxide. These pollutants lead to which environmental problem?

a. Denitrification
b. Acid rain
c. Global climate change
d. Ozone depletion

138. What lab equipment would most likely be used to measure a liquid solution?

a. Flask
b. Triple beam balance
c. Graduated cylinder
d. Test tube

139. During a chemistry experiment, which of the data below would not be collected for your lab report?

a. Temperature changes
b. Color changes
c. Production of gas or odor
d. Observations of other trials

140. A teacher tells the class about a new drug that is being tested on 200 volunteer subjects. Half the volunteers are given the new drug while the other half are given a harmless sugar pill. The volunteers who are given the sugar pill serve as the:

a. Control group
b. Experimental group
c. Variable
d. Indicator

Mathematics

141. The ratio of employee wages and benefits to all other operational costs of a business is 2: 3. If a business's total operating expenses are $130,000 per month, how much money does the company spend on employee wages and benefits?

a. $43,333.33
b. $86,666.67
c. $52,000.00
d. $78,000.00

142. Tom needs to buy ink cartridges and printer paper. Each ink cartridge costs \$30. Each ream of paper costs \$5. He has \$100 to spend. Which of the following inequalities may be used to find the combinations of ink cartridges and printer paper that he may purchase?

a. $30c + 5p \leq 100$
b. $30c + 5p < 100$
c. $30c + 5p > 100$
d. $30c + 5p \geq 100$

143. Mr. Amad draws a line with a slope of $-\frac{2}{3}$ on the white board through three points. Which of the sets could possibly be these three points?

a. $(-6,-2), (-7,-4), (-8,-6)$
b. $(-4,7), (-8,13), (-6,10)$
c. $(-3,-1), (-6,1), (0,-3)$
d. $(-2,-3), (-1,-3), (0,-3)$

144. Marcus is mowing yards and doing odd jobs to earn money for a new video game system that costs \$325. Marcus only charges \$6.50 per hour. Which of the following equations represents the number of hours Marcus needs to work to earn \$325?

a. $6.50x = 325$
b. $6.50 + x = 325$
c. $325x = 6.50$
d. $6.50x + 325 = x$

145. What is the constant of proportionality represented by the table below?

x	y
2	−8
5	−20
7	−28
10	−40
11	−44

a. −12
b. −8
c. −6
d. −4

146. Which of the following solids has the smallest volume?

a. A cube with side length 5 cm
b. A rectangular prism with height 5 cm, length 3 cm, and width 7 cm
c. A cylinder with height 4 cm and radius 3 cm
d. A cone with height 10 cm and radius 3 cm

147. Which of the following describes how to find the volume of a regular solid prism?

a. Find the perimeter of the base of the prism and multiply by the height of the prism.
b. Find the area of the base of the prism and multiply by the height of the prism.
c. Find the sum of the areas of the faces and multiply by the length of the prism.
d. Find the sum of the areas of the lateral faces and multiply by the number of faces.

148. Which of the following best represents the value of x, shown in the triangle below?

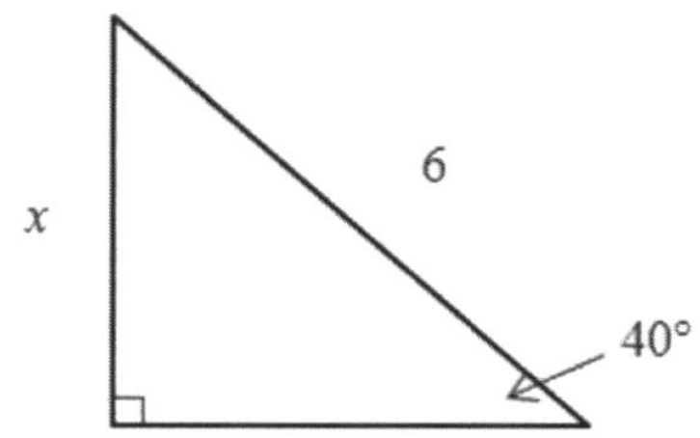

a. 2.6
b. 3.1
c. 3.9
d. 4.4

149. A man standing on a flat, level surface casts a shadow that is 6.2 ft in length. The man is 5.8 ft tall. Which of the following best represents the distance from the top of his head to the end of the shadow?

a. 7 ft
b. 7.5 ft
c. 8 ft
d. 8.5 ft

150. Which of the following transformations has been applied to ΔABC?

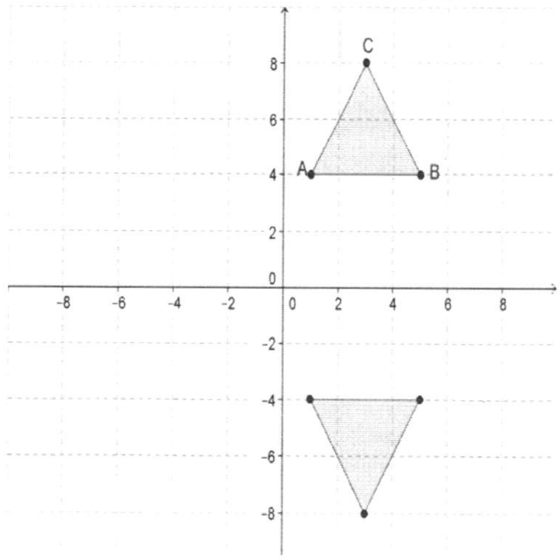

a. Translation
b. Rotation of 90 degrees
c. Reflection
d. Dilation

151. Which of the following represents 47,800?

a. 4.78×10^{-4}
b. 4.78×10^{-3}
c. 4.78×10^{3}
d. 4.78×10^{4}

152. Which of the following illustrates the additive inverse property?

a. The sum of a and 0 is a.
b. The sum of a and $-a$ is 0.
c. The sum of a and a is $2a$.
d. The sum of a and any variable x is $a + x$.

153. Which of the following illustrates the commutative property of multiplication?

a. The product of a and b is ab.
b. The product of a and 0 is 0.
c. The product of a and $-a$ is $-a^2$.
d. The product of a and b is the same as the product of b and a.

154. Which of the following statements is true?

a. The set of whole numbers is a subset of the set of natural numbers.
b. The set of integers is a subset of the set of natural numbers.
c. The set of integers is a subset of the set of rational numbers.
d. The set of rational numbers is a subset of the set of integers.

155. In a town of 35,638 people, about a quarter of the population is under the age of 35. Of those, just over a third attend local K–12 schools. If the number of students in each grade is about the same, how many fourth graders likely reside in the town?

a. Fewer than 100
b. Between 200 and 300
c. Between 300 and 400
d. More than 400

156. $5/6 \div 3/7 \times 5/9 =$

a. 6/5
b. 11/6
c. 135/129
d. 175/162

157. Which of the following correctly represents the expanded form of 0.593?

a. $5 \times \frac{1}{10^0} + 9 \times \frac{1}{10^1} + 3 \times \frac{1}{10^2}$
b. $5 \times \frac{1}{10^2} + 9 \times \frac{1}{10^3} + 3 \times \frac{1}{10^4}$
c. $5 \times \frac{1}{10^3} + 9 \times \frac{1}{10^2} + 3 \times \frac{1}{10^1}$
d. $5 \times \frac{1}{10^1} + 9 \times \frac{1}{10^2} + 3 \times \frac{1}{10^3}$

158. Quentin sets aside 10% of his monthly salary to save for a car. If his monthly salary is $2,450, how much will he set aside each month?

a. $2.45
b. $24.50
c. $245
d. $2,450

159. Ben's current monthly rent is $750. He is moving to another apartment complex, where the monthly rent will be $900. What is the percent increase in his monthly rent amount?

a. 15%
b. 17.5%
c. 19.25%
d. 20%

160. Which of the following options represents equivalency between different representations of rational numbers?

a. $16 \div (6-4)^2 = 64$
b. $8 - 2(7-4) = 18$
c. $2^3 \div 2 - 2(2) = 0$
d. $2 + 3(2^2) = 20$

161. Elisha spins a spinner with 8 equally spaced sections labeled 1–8. What is the probability that the spinner lands either on a number greater than 5 or on 2?

a. $\frac{1}{2}$
b. $\frac{1}{8}$
c. $\frac{3}{8}$
d. $\frac{3}{64}$

162. Suppose two variables show a correlation of 0.9. Which of the following statements BEST describes the relationship?

a. The variables show a strong correlation.
b. The variables show some correlation, but it is neither weak nor strong.
c. The variables show a weak correlation.
d. The variables show a perfect correlation.

163. Which of the following correlation coefficients represents a weak correlation?

a. −0.9
b. 0.2
c. −0.7
d. 0.8

164. A certain special die has eight sides instead of six. The probability of rolling an odd number is:

a. The same as for a six-sided die
b. One-third more than for a six-sided die
c. One-third less than for a six-sided die
d. 25% greater

165. Kayla rolls a die and tosses a coin. What is the probability she gets an even number and heads?

a. $\frac{1}{6}$
b. $\frac{1}{4}$
c. $\frac{1}{3}$
d. 1

166. What is accurate regarding manipulative objects that can help young children learn math concepts?

a. Teachers can find many math manipulatives for sale, and/or can make their own homemade ones.
b. Teachers can only find helpful math manipulatives by buying those made by expert manufacturers.
c. Teachers will save money and attain much greater learning benefits by hand-making manipulatives.
d. Teachers should not waste money buying, or time making, these as children learn more from ideas.

167. Which of the following is most accurate regarding young children's development of numeracy skills?

a. Young children typically learn all of the number names before they learn to count.
b. Young children typically learn to name all of the numbers and count simultaneously.
c. Young children typically learn to count before they have learned all number names.
d. Young children typically learn these two numeracy skills in individually varying order.

168. Which of the following goals is appropriate in the category of algebraic reasoning for first-grade students?

a. Students represent one- and two-step problems involving addition and subtraction of whole numbers to 1,000 using pictorial models, number lines, and equations.
b. Students represent real-world relationships using number pairs in a table and verbal descriptions.
c. Students represent word problems involving addition and subtraction of whole numbers up to 20 using concrete and pictorial models and number sentences.
d. Students recite numbers up to at least 100 by ones and tens beginning with any given number.

169. Which of these is true about having an awareness of patterns and relationships in the real world?

a. It does not inform our understanding of the basic structure of things.
b. It helps us understand series of events, but not predict future ones.
c. It is unrelated to our basic feeling of confidence in the environment.
d. It increases our self-efficacy about interacting with our environment.

170. Miss Wise asks her students to work in pairs to construct Venn diagrams which classify rational numbers, irrational numbers, real numbers, and integers. As she walks around the room to observe their progress, which of the following criterion could she use to assess the students' understanding of these sets of numbers?

a. The set of integers should include the other three sets.
b. The set of rational numbers should include the other three sets.
c. The set of irrational numbers should include the other three sets.
d. The set of real numbers should include the other three sets.

171. A 6th grade math teacher is introducing the concept of positive and negative numbers to a group of students. Which of the following models would be the most effective when introducing this concept?

a. Fraction strips
b. Venn diagrams
c. Shaded regions
d. Number lines

172. Which of these is true about the use of manipulatives for EC math learning?

a. Manipulatives are so effective for learning that some early math curricula require these.
b. Manipulatives help preschoolers with visual/haptic learning styles but not other children.
c. Manipulatives can help preschoolers learn concrete things rather than abstract concepts.
d. Manipulatives are fun, but preschoolers do not learn by seeing/touching/moving objects.

173. Which of these is correct regarding young children and the measurement of time?

a. Young children typically develop an understanding of the abstract concept of time very early.
b. Adults should not refer to periods of time with young children before they understand them.
c. Using activities involving counting allows children to generalize these to the counting of time.
d. Adults can say "yesterday, today, tomorrow" with young children and they will understand it.

174. Suppose that a child in a preschool learning center enjoys sorting different rocks by color. Which of the following teacher practices is the best example of emphasis on connecting the informal math activity with formal math vocabulary?

a. Telling the child s/he is classifying the rocks
b. Asking the child how s/he is sorting the rocks
c. Asking after s/he finishes other ways to sort
d. These all exemplify the vocabulary emphasis

175. While informally observing students as they complete a worksheet on one-to-one correspondence, a kindergarten teacher notices that one student is repeating numbers as he counts. Which of the following instructional materials would be effective in strengthening the student's understanding of this concept?

a. A number line
b. Pattern blocks
c. Base-10 blocks
d. A counting mat

Answer Key and Explanations for Test #1

Language Arts and Reading

1. C: The fact that digital networking enables educators and learners to communicate nearly instantly with a variety of experts, mentors, and peers all over the world has transformed the social interactions available in the educational community. Additional advantages of digital networking include that digital educational resources can be linked to one another; that embedded hyperlinks afford students easy access to learning supports like electronic notepads, graphic organizers, supplementary information, reading comprehension prompts, encyclopedias, dictionaries and thesauruses, and more; and that the diversity of digital formats available provide experiences more similar in their diversity to that of individual students. These advantages are all transformative of learning itself. Access to global communications is an advantage transformative specifically of social interactions (including remote and long-distance) within the learning process, as well as of learning.

2. D: Having classmates offer peer reviews (A), having the teacher evaluate their work (B), and comparing their work to that of their classmates (C) are all valuable sources of feedback for students about their performance and progress in speaking and enacting through oral reports and presentations as they give different perspectives; however, video recordings of student performance (D) are the only type of completely objective feedback among these choices because they provide an exact record of what the student did. This enables students to self-monitor, make changes/improvements, and appreciate their own progress over time.

3. C: The students have been instructed to read the documents quickly, looking for key words in order to gather the basic premise of each. Skimming allows a reader to quickly gain a broad understanding of a piece of writing in order to determine if a more thorough reading is warranted. Skimming allows students who are researching a topic on the internet or in print to consider a substantial body of information in order to select only that of particular relevance.

4. D: Nonverbal behaviors during speeches influence the listeners' perceptions of the speaker's competence, good character, trustworthiness, and therefore credibility. Speakers should make eye contact with everybody in the audience, not just certain listeners (A). Their body movements should not be random or unrelated (B) to what they are saying (e.g., pacing, face rubbing, playing with one's hair, tapping pencils or toes, etc.), but they should reinforce their verbal messages. Facial expressions should not be startling or unexpected (C); they should be consistent with both the verbal content and the speaker's vocal tones. A speaker's gestures should also be congruent with the meaning (D) of what s/he is saying, to fit with and emphasize the points they are communicating.

5. B: Relational messages, as opposed to content messages, are concerned with the relationship between a speaker and a recipient rather than with the overt subject of the communication. They may convey belonging, respect, or disapproval, among other things. They are frequently largely or entirely nonverbal; because of this, they may be supported with verbal feedback to confirm them. The content of the message, "Should I come over after work?" is a logistical request. If a speaker leans forward to touch a recipient who is weeping, the relational message is "Do you need my support?" The recipient might respond with a nod and a grateful look, or might clarify the speaker's offer by saying, "I won't be good company, but you can come."

6. B: Slogans are catchphrases that advertisers want consumers to remember and associate with their brands. They are generally reinforced through repetition. Pathos is a persuasive technique that involves appeals to emotion. A bandwagon appeal advises using a brand because everybody else does (i.e., through popularity/peer pressure). A testimonial is a statement by someone (usually a celebrity or other consumer) endorsing/supporting a brand.

7. D: This description involves both an expert opinion (a) because the woman is identified as a doctor who recommends the prescription and a testimonial (b) because this doctor also identifies herself as a satisfied user of the product. It does not involve a bandwagon (c) appeal, which cites use of a brand by a majority of consumers to persuade others to join them.

8. B: The teacher used an informal reading inventory to gain insight into the students' abilities in a larger group setting. While some informal reading inventories, or IRIs, are administered between one teacher and one student, these inventories usually work best in a group setting. The benefit of this type of assessment is that it provides insight within the context of an entire class or large group in a short period of time. This assessment does not provide specific or generalized information about the students' progress, but rather allows the teacher to gauge her students' needs at any given point during instruction.

9. B: Spelling is often taught in a systematic way. Students receive words and memorize them for quizzes and tests. However, spelling is related to many aspects of language and must be treated as a dynamic subject. Integrating the words into other parts of language instruction will help students not only learn how to spell correctly, but also to recall meanings of words and various rules of English spelling and grammar. By using the same words in different subjects, the students will retain the information more readily than if they study the words intensely for one week in only one context.

10. B: The LEA lets children use their own life experiences in constructing stories, and enables them to use their own words in composing these. In this method, children are not interacting with published text in books (A) but creating their own. The LEA teaches beginning reading. When it is applied with young children, they are not writing down the stories they compose (C), the teacher is. They are not reading books aloud to the teacher (D); rather, they are dictating to a teacher, who transcribes what they say. Teachers and children then review the story they have created, and the teacher has recorded, together.

11. D: For writing, teachers should instruct their students to think about what kinds of proof and/or evidence they will need to provide for their readers to agree with their points (A). They should instruct students to consider not only what points they will make in writing that their readers might agree with, but moreover what points their readers are likely to disagree with (B), and how to refute or counter those disagreements to persuade skeptical audiences. Teachers should have students think about what information their readers already know and what information they will share with their readers (C). They should additionally instruct students to consider what information they and their readers share in common (D).

12. B: Questionnaires (A) typically use short-answer items such as yes/no questions/statements, Likert scales measuring within a range of agreement/disagreement, or like/dislike rather than open-ended requests for reflective comments or feedback. Having students rate teachers (C) is inappropriate because the focus is on curriculum and assessment design and use, not on a teacher's performance. Assigning essays (D) is more likely to obtain students writing about the subject matter itself rather than their reflective responses. Having students write in journals (B) enables them to reflect on their course matter and tests and record these reflections, which teachers can then read.

13. B: The topics of cooperative projects and/or discussions and whether they are age-appropriate in difficulty relate most to cognitive developmental levels, i.e., what they can understand. Social developmental levels (A) relate to whether students can interact effectively in peer groups. Emotional developmental levels (C) relate to student emotional intelligence, i.e., emotional self-management plus sensitivity to, understanding of, and appropriate response to others' emotions. Behavioral developmental levels (D) relate to whether students can regulate their behaviors appropriately within peer groups.

14. C: Lexile measures assign numbers to many books and articles that identify their reading levels, from below 200L to above 1700L. These are reading levels not to be confused with grade levels. Students can also be assigned Lexile measure numbers through their scores on standardized reading tests they may be given in school. Teachers and students can select texts that correspond to a range around a student's Lexile measure; 50L above and 100L below the student's number is a recommended range. Lexile measures do not find these texts; teachers and/or students do. They are not advised to find only texts exactly matching a student's number, as this would overly restrict available reading material and is unnecessary. Students can generally read and enjoy texts in a range around their level. Lexile measures are not assigned to every book and article published; over 80 million articles and over 100,000 books have Lexile measure numbers, providing identification of ample reading matter for those wishing to use this system.

15. C: Summative assessments are administered after instruction and less often than formative assessments, which teachers make more frequently during instruction (A) to inform changes to make their teaching more effective (B). Typical times for summative assessments are after each lesson, unit, and school year is completed (C). Teachers rely on formative, not summative assessments for individual student data (D); they rely on summative assessment results for group data and group comparisons.

16. A: In order to achieve a balanced language program, a teacher must spend time on many different skills that have been mentioned in previous questions and answers. Language skills cannot be reduced to the process of reading (fluency plus comprehension). Students develop their language skills over a long period of time, and they do so across multiple domains. Students' ability to listen and speak, write, view, respond, synthesize information, and read for a variety of purposes all must be included in daily instruction. By practicing only fluency and comprehension, students will not fully understand the various functions of language skills and may even lack an appreciation for them.

17. D: Collaborative Strategic Reading (CSR) is a technique that largely depends on cooperative learning and practice of metacognition. In practice, this look slike putting students into groups and having them self-monitor their own reading comprehension using various reading strategies. One popular reading strategy that can be used includes "click and clunk," which is where students report which parts of the story *click* to them, or which makes sense without much difficulty, and which parts *clunk*, or are not easy to understand. Then the group would collaborate to resolve the clunks and ensure everyone understood the reading assignment. Other strategies can include use of context clues, rereading, or any other reading comprehension strategy, paired with group discussion.

18. B: There are many, many factors that affect reading comprehension in various proportions, depending on the student. Generally speaking, students must be able to recognize vocabulary, decode unfamiliar words, and monitor their own understanding in order to comprehend a given text. In Choice A, all of these factors could affect comprehension; written language development and breakfast, however, are probably less important than the set of factors in Choice B. In Choice C, the factors seem to relate primarily to a student's understanding of the words in the text—vocabulary, sight words, and the ability to look up words. However, students must understand more than simply the words on the page; they must understand the relationships between the words and the underlying meaning of the whole text. In Choice D, classroom participation and performance in other subjects does not necessarily indicate or affect comprehension skills.

19. B: Fluency requires good decoding skills. Fluent readers do not frequently stumble when encountering unfamiliar words; rather, they use their decoding skills and phonemic awareness to effectively associate letters and sounds. The other choices describe some of the defining characteristics of fluency.

20. A: One teaching technique that is effective for promoting print awareness in young children is to have them narrate books that contain only pictures. This is even more effective when teachers reinforce the activity by providing a directly related reward, such as having them eat pancakes after they narrate the picture book *Pancakes.* Even with young children who cannot read yet, it is good to read to them from large-print books (B) that they can more easily view, facilitating their beginning to learn to read sooner. Teachers should label objects and areas in their classrooms using both pictures and words together (C) to teach and reinforce correspondences between spoken and written words. Storybooks teachers read to preschoolers should use predictable, familiar words (D).

21. A: Letter–sound correspondence relies on the relationship between a spoken sound or group of sounds and the letters conventionally used in English to write them.

22. A: Emergent readers are those who are not yet reading fluently (with appropriate speed and accuracy). Choice B refers to the practice of reviewing relationships between letters and sounds, which is vital to building reading skills. Choice C would help students build vocabulary retention by requiring them to find unfamiliar words in the dictionary. This practice causes the student to analyze and retain spelling of unfamiliar words, as well as reinforces dictionary/reference skills. Choice D addresses the fact that many words in the English language are irregularly spelled and cannot be decoded with conventional phonetic instruction. While invented spelling described in Choice A may be permitted in emergent readers, this practice is not likely to build specific reading skills.

23. C: Among categories of phonological awareness activities, working with rhymes is less difficult than others. Within the rhyming category, the easiest activity for children is to identify which words they hear rhyme with each other. The second easiest rhyme activity is being able to discriminate rhyming from non-rhyming words by picking which words in a list rhyme (B). The hardest rhyme activity is creating rhymes by naming words that rhyme with a word that is given (A). Therefore, these are not all equally difficult (D).

24. C: While *some* children's reading lacks fluency due to deficits in their word-decoding abilities, this is not *always* (A) the case: some children simply need more reading practice to develop fluency. Children's motivation to read (B) *is* affected by their reading fluency: when reading is laborious, children do not enjoy it and avoid reading; when reading is easy, children enjoy it and want to read. Fluency has much *greater* impact (D) on the performance of students in higher grades, when the volume of reading required of them in school is exponentially greater.

25. A: An effective way to teach students the difference between denotation and connotation is to provide example sentences and have students choose a given word that best expresses the connotation of a highlighted word in each sentence. For example, to show the connotation of the word *challenge*, an example sentence "This is one of the many challenges that must be faced in order to solve the problem" could be given, and students could choose whether the connotation suggested by "challenges" in this case was "threats," "obstacles," "criticisms," or "setbacks." This instructional strategy is summarized in choice A, which is the correct answer. Since words generally have denotations and may or may not have connotations depending on their use, a Venn diagram would be misleading, and choice B is incorrect. Choice C is also incorrect, as highlighting words in a passage would not require students to distinguish between denotations and connotations, nor even to identify the exact connotations of words in context. Choice D would not be logical, since not all words have an emotional connotation, and the definition alone will be of little use for determining the connotations of a specific use of a word.

26. B: Cloze sentences are sentences with certain words or phrases from a given text replaced with blanks. They allow students to fill in the blanks and thereby use a reasoning process to learn the meanings of terms. This type of activity would be the most effective of those listed in the other answer choices for helping students understand the text and the terms it presents, so choice B is correct. Summarizing may be helpful, but it would not target specific terms, as cloze sentences would, so choice A is incorrect. Creative extension would help in applying the concepts one they are learned, but it would not be possible until the concepts are learned, so choice C is incorrect. Rote memorization would not enable students to use reasoning, so it would not necessarily be an aid to understanding the text or the terms, so choice D is incorrect.

27. D: When students ask themselves how the information in a text they are reading fits with what they already know, they are relating the text to their own prior knowledge, which increases their reading comprehension. Students should not only ask themselves what kinds of "expert questions" fit the subject matter of the text (A)—e.g., classification, physical, and chemical properties are typical question topics in science; genre, character, plot, and theme are typical of literature questions; sequence, cause-and-effect, and comparison-contrast questions are typical of history—but also what questions the material brings up for them personally (B). It is necessary and important for students to ask themselves continually how each text portion relates to its chapter's main ideas (C) as they read to optimize their reading comprehension and retention.

28. A: Prefixes and suffixes are important for reading comprehension because they change the meanings of the root word to which they are attached. A student who understands that *un* means "not" will be able to decipher the meanings of words such as *unwanted, unhappy,* or *unreasonable.*

29. B: Teachers should apply a variety of instructional techniques to enable students with different strengths, needs, and learning styles to understand sound-letter and letter-word relationships, but they should not restrict the instructional modalities to auditory and visual (A) simply because sounds are auditory and letters are visual. Multisensory modalities (B) are more effective because different students use different senses to learn; redundancy is necessary for learning; and input to multiple senses affords a more multidimensional learning experience, promoting comprehension and retention. While some aspects of this instruction should be consistent (e.g., starting with high-frequency letters and with phonemes children can produce more easily), sticking to only one method and set of materials (C) prevents using variety to reach all students. Visually similar letters and auditorily similar phonemes should *not* be introduced together (D) before students can discriminate among them; teachers should begin with more obvious differences.

30. D: The ideal group for guided reading consists of five or six students. Because students' needs and abilities vary, small and flexible groupings allow students to interact most effectively with the teacher and with each other. Reading aloud and developing fluency are major components of the guided reading experience.

31. B: Students predicting what will happen in a text helps to support active reading by creating expectations for the text and the desire to see these expectations met (A). Summarizing current knowledge can activate what students already know, which can lead to better engagement because students may see the opportunity to learn more (C). Looking ahead and coming up with questions the text may answer combines these two concepts, prompting students to form expectations and identify what they hope to learn (D). Drawing a story map after reading is useful, but drawing one of predictions made before reading would go into too much depth about ideas that may not even be in the text. This is least likely to be effective in supporting active reading, making choice B correct.

32. D: According to the National Reading Panel (NRP, 2000), multiple and replicated research studies conducted over time confirm that systematic phonics instruction is most effective when taught as part of a comprehensive reading program that also includes phonemic awareness, vocabulary, reading fluency, and reading comprehension. Hence teaching phonics separately or only with phonemic awareness are incorrect. The research also finds this instruction effective for both K-6 students and students having difficulty with learning to read.

33. A: A phoneme is a unit of language that represents the smallest unit of sound. For instance, the *k* in *kit* or the *ph* in *graph* both represent English phonemes. Graphemes are written phonemes and can be alphabetic letters, numbers, characters, punctuation marks, and so on. Neither phonemes nor graphemes have semantic meaning unless they are used as part of a larger unit of language, such as the morpheme. Morphemes can be roots, prefixes, and suffixes. The word *rechargeable* is comprised of three morphemes: *re*, *charge*, and *able*. Each component of this word has a meaning unto itself, but when combined with the others, each one is used to make a new word with a new meaning.

34. D: Phonemes are the smallest units of sound in words. In this activity, students are replacing one phoneme with another, which is known as phoneme substitution. Alliteration refers to a series of words in which most words begin with the same sound. Segmenting refers to breaking a word down into its individual sounds, or phonemes. Onset and rime blending involve blending the beginning sound of a word with the rest of the word.

35. C: According to the Association of College and Research Libraries, information literacy is the set of skills that an individual must have for the finding, retrieval, analysis, and use of information. While it is required for reading and understanding information, it is required for more than this, so choice A is incorrect. It does not necessarily or exclusively involve retaining a lot of information or communicating information effectively, so choices B and D are incorrect. Rather, information literacy involves knowing how to find information, how to evaluate information critically, and how to apply information judiciously to meet specific purposes.

36. C: Class composition and preferences. Before selecting literature for the classroom, the teacher needs to assess the class, considering where they are with their reading skills and what their current interests are. After determining these things, the teacher would next evaluate books that seem appropriate for this particular group of children in terms of plot, character, and reading level.

37. A: This describes the poetic form of haiku, which originated in Japanese poetic tradition and has been adopted by other languages. Though Japanese haiku can be translated for meaning, doing so generally necessitates different numbers of syllables. American poet Ezra Pound's 1911 poem "In a Station of the Metro" is sometimes viewed as an early example of haiku being adopted in English. The poem reads:

> *The apparition of these faces in the crowd:*
> *Petals on a wet, black bough.*

Sonnets, limericks, and cinquains are all poetic forms with well-defined structures, but they have their own rules for meter and do not follow the five-seven-five syllabification of haiku.

38. C: To select materials suitable for partner (paired) reading, the teacher should identify materials that are suitable for the *lower* reader's instructional reading level, not the higher reader's. Instructional level equals no more than one reading error per 10 words. Remember, the lower independent reading level is no more than one reading error per 20 words. Each student partner in a pair should read the *same* passage from the same text, not different ones to enable modeling by the more fluent reader for the lower reader and repeated reading. The teacher should select enough reading materials for every pair of students to read two new passages each week.

39. A: The plot of a story is a set of events, and each event is impacted by a conflict that a character in the story is experiencing. Thus, conflict drives the plot of the story forward, and there cannot be a plot without some kind of conflict. Choice B is incorrect because, in most stories, the protagonist's goal is to resolve the main conflict. In fact, for many protagonists, their personal goals or troubles contribute to or form the main conflict. Choice C is incorrect because the impact that each type of conflict has on the plot depends on the story. Choice D is incorrect because the main conflict is generally resolved in the climax of a plot, not before it.

40. B: Fantasy stories and books revolve around magical or supernatural creatures. Science fiction is a similar genre, but it relies on the portrayal of a future world, creatures from other planets or galaxies, etc. The action and adventure genre typically involves heroic characters in dangerous and exciting scenarios, such as solving a mystery or journeying through an unfamiliar environment. Historical fiction stories are set sometime in the past and are usually accurate in their historical information.

41. C: Full reading comprehension of informational text depends on both the reader's ability to recall information or prior knowledge and the reader's ability to make inferences based on that information and the text. Therefore, choice C is correct, and choices A, B, and D are incorrect.

42. A: In both the fictional narrative genre and the nonfictional informational genre, the author will demonstrate some individual writing style; even very factual and objective expositional writing will reveal some personal stylistic characteristics. Labeled diagrams and photos are more likely to be found in informational nonfiction. The majority of books with excitement and drama are fictional narratives (some informational nonfiction books are presented in narrative form and include excitement, especially in children's literature, but these are the minority). Themes and plots are also literary elements associated with fictional narrative.

43. A: Choice A is correct as evaluation (i.e., making critical judgments about some information) commonly incorporates the processes that the other answer choices refer to and is therefore more complex than they are. Application (B) requires taking information learned and using it in new or different circumstances. Comprehension (C) requires showing understanding of the information learned. Knowledge recall (D) involves showing proficiency in information learned.

44. B: When teachers assign cooperative writing partnerships, each student in a pair should not always take only one role (A); they must both take turns writing and reviewing their partner's writing (B) to experience both roles in the process. Each student should provide not only positive feedback (C) or only constructive feedback (D) to a partner, but both. For example, if the assignment is using descriptive adjectives, positive feedback would be identifying specific descriptive adjectives the partner used; constructive feedback could be identifying sentences that could use more descriptive adjectives.

45. D: According to research-based writing instruction strategies, when teachers assign students to small collaborative writing groups, they should set individual performance expectations for within-group as well as individual work. Teachers should also support student groups by providing them with structure. Classmates in collaborative writing groups should give each other both positive feedback for reinforcement and constructive feedback for correction as well.

46. C: Mnemonic devices help with remembering key sets of information by organizing it into patterns. For example, many mnemonic devices are made by identifying a series of initial letters corresponding to the words that must be remembered but forming an easily remembered acronym or phrase using the same initial letters (such as "RAFT" or "Role, Audience, Format, Topic" to help students remember the key elements of a writing assignment). The other answer choices reflect devices that are useful for reading and writing but are not specifically used for remembering key sets of information. Making outlines (A) helps with identifying main ideas and supporting details and organizing them into a hierarchy. Checklists (B) help ensure one has completed all steps or components of a task or project. Graphic organizers (D) help with visually representing abstract concepts and relationships.

47. A: Considering audience is not necessary in order to determine purpose, so choice A is correct. Choice B is incorrect because writers should use audience and purpose to decide on the best structure and organization for those who will read the writing. Choice C is incorrect, as audience, along with purpose of writing, will determine what style and tone to use in a piece of writing, and will therefore affect word choice. Identifying an audience will also help in choosing specific words that will be most understandable and appealing to readers. Finally, choice D is incorrect because audience will also dictate how much time to spend on research. Some readers will expect more supporting evidence, while others will not.

48. C: The headings and subheadings of a topic outline are words or phrases, and it is brief. The headings and subheadings of a sentence outline are full sentences, and it is longer and more detailed.

49. C: Students are more involved in their writing if the audience varies. Examples of varied audiences include letters to the editor, letters to a friend, an essay written for a community group, and a story written for younger children or beginning readers.

50. D: Among these major types of conflicts found in literary plots, only one is an internal conflict, while the other three are external conflicts. Choice D, man against himself, is classified as an internal conflict because it goes on inside a character's mind. Man against man (A), man against nature (B), and man against society (C) are all classified as external conflicts because they involve a struggle between a character and someone or something outside that character.

Social Science

51. C: If a country's currency increases in value, foreigners will have to give up more of their own currency to get the original country's currency in order to buy the original country's goods and services. This will cause a drop in exports. At the same time, it will be less expensive for people in the original country to exchange their currency for foreign currencies, causing the price of imported goods to drop and the total value of imports to rise.

52. B: Marx's focus in *The Communist Manifesto* (1848) and *Das Kapital* (1867) was on the inevitable conflict between the working class and the capitalists who own the means of production. He identified these two opposing forces as the proletariat and the bourgeoisie.

53. B: There was not a reduction in military spending after the war. Although the manufacturing demand for war supplies and the size of the military decreased, the government had increased military spending from $10 billion in 1947 to more than $50 billion by 1953—a more than fivefold increase. This increase strengthened the American economy. Other factors contributing to the strengthened economy included the significantly higher birth rates during the Baby Boom from 1946 to 1957, which stimulated the growth of the building and automotive industries by increased demand. Government programs, such as the GI Bill (the Servicemen's Readjustment Act of 1944), other veterans' benefits, and the National Defense Education Act all encouraged college enrollments, which increased by nearly four times. Additionally, larger families, increased mobility and low-interest loans offered to veterans led to suburban development and growth as well as increased home construction. Improvements in public health were also results of the new affluence; the rate of infant deaths decreased significantly, and as a result, from 1946–1957, the American life span rose from 67 to 71 years. Moreover, Dr. Jonas Salk developed the polio vaccine in 1955, which virtually wiped out poliomyelitis, preventing many deaths and disabilities in children.

54. B: Economists understand the true cost of an action as not only its monetary cost but the cost of other opportunities missed as a result of pursuing that action. For example, if a person chooses to go to school rather than working, the cost of the action involves not only tuition and other associated fees and expenses, but the money one would have earned working, as well as the time one could have spent pursuing other activities. The concept of opportunity cost is not described by options (A), (C), or (D), each of which is concerned only with monetary costs. Each of these answers can be rejected on that basis.

55. D: The education of the workforce generally is not treated as a separate, direct input in the basic model of GDP. GDP refers to the value of all goods and services produced by a country in a specific timeframe, and basic models describe that output as depending directly on inputs like labor, capital, and technology. The education of its workforce can impact the quantity of output by increasing worker productivity, but it is usually considered part of labor quality (human capital) rather than a standalone input. GDP is more directly impacted by the size of the workforce, the amount of a country's capital, and the technology already in place. The size of the workforce implies that there are people who are ready and willing to work. The amount of capital means that there is a sufficient number of factories and assets available to create goods and services. Technology refers to the methods, processes, and tools that help labor and capital produce more efficiently.

56. C: A person who has taken out a fixed-rate loan can benefit from inflation by paying back the loan with dollars that are less valuable than they were when the loan was taken out. In the other examples, inflation harms the individual or entity.

57. B: John Maynard Keynes argued that government could help revitalize a recessionary economy by increasing government spending and therefore increasing aggregate demand. This is known as demand-side economics.

58. A: Economics is defined as the study of scarcity, the situation in which resources are limited and wants are unlimited.

59. B: Tropical regions near the Equator tend to experience relatively constant temperatures year-round because the angle at which sunlight hits them remains relatively constant throughout the year. In regions that are farther north or south, the angle at which sunlight hits them changes much more drastically due to the changing angle of the Earth's axis relative to the Sun. This results in greater variations in the length of daylight and in temperatures. Tropical regions do have seasons (usually a "wet" season and a "dry" season), but temperature fluctuations are less pronounced than those in regions farther from the Equator.

60. A: Both rural and urban areas grew in population numbers, making choices C and D incorrect, but urban areas grew by a much larger margin. This best supports the statement that rural to urban migration was a probable trend. Choice B is incorrect because urban to rural migration would likely lead to significantly higher rural population numbers.

61. B: The C horizon of soil consists of weathered rock. A soil that has been in the same place for a long time will begin to develop unique layers known as horizons. The bottom layer is called the R horizon; it consists of unweathered bedrock. Just above is the C horizon, which is composed of weathered rock fragments. Next up is the B horizon, made up of minerals and drier soil. Above that is the A horizon, or topsoil, which has a great deal of organic matter in it. The top layer is known as the O horizon. It is a thin layer of humus.

62. B: Latitudes are lines that run east and west on geographical maps, and are also called parallels. Longitudes (A) are lines that run north and south, so longitude is not a synonym for latitude. Longitudes are also called meridians (C), so meridian is a synonym for longitude, not latitude. Coordinates (D) are the numbers of degrees assigned to various longitudes and latitudes.

63. D: Alaska is the largest state in terms of area. It is about 660,000 square miles, while the second-largest state, Texas, is about 270,000 square miles. Despite its immensity, however, Alaska is sparsely populated, with fewer than 630,000 permanent residents. Much of the state is covered in ice year round, and there are several months during the winter in which the sun barely rises at all. Nevertheless, Alaska is an incredible source of natural resources for the continental United States. In particular, Alaska supplies large amounts of oil, timber, and fish to the rest of the nation. There is a continuous conflict between environmentalists and those who want to harvest the state's natural resources more aggressively.

64. C: Physical geography focuses on processes and patterns in the natural environment. What people eat in any given geographic region is largely dependent on such environmental factors as climate and the availability of arable land. Religion, family, and language may all be affected by geographical factors, but they are not as immediately affected as dietary preferences.

65. D: The scale would be largest on a map of Greenwich Village. Scale is described as large when it is closer to life-sized; the smaller the region being depicted, the closer to actual size the map can be. Of the four answer choices, Greenwich Village, a neighborhood in Manhattan, is the smallest. Therefore, it must be depicted in the largest scale. Incidentally, Benelux is the name for the region of northern Europe that includes Belgium, the Netherlands, and Luxembourg.

66. B: There are four intermediate directions. They are northwest, northeast, southwest, and southeast. The intermediate directions are midway between each set of adjacent cardinal directions. The cardinal directions are north, south, east, and west. On a compass rose, the cardinal directions are typically indicated by large points, while the intermediate directions are represented by smaller points.

67. C: The Federalist Party advocated a pro-British foreign policy and therefore opposed the War of 1812. This made the Federalists unpopular with many Americans; this unpopularity deepened when the war ended after several American victories. The Federalist Party did advocate a strong central government; however, this position was not a key factor in the Party's decline. This eliminates option D. Option A can be rejected because the Federalist Party did organize state political parties in states such as Connecticut, Delaware, and Maryland. Many members of the Federalist Party were pro-trade and pro-business, as many members were well-to-do businessmen. This eliminates option B.

68. B: Despite the constitutional guarantee of free speech, it is not absolute. There are certain restrictions in which laws regulate defamation, slander, libel, conspiracy, and occasions when speech has the potential of causing "imminent harm." During the Vietnam War era, draftees would publicize their displeasure by burning their draft cards—this action actually constituted a federal crime. School employees are required to be socially responsible and are liable to discipline if their actions encourage delinquency or profanity. The laws prohibit threats against the President only when it represents a real threat, not "political hyperbole."

69. C: Thomas Jefferson embraced John Locke's concept of separation of church and state. Deism posits that a Supernatural force created the world and universe, but that He did not intervene after creation. Jefferson wanted minimal central governing, just as he viewed the Creator's relationship with the universe.

70. C: The main subject matter of civic responsibility is a person's responsibilities as a citizen. By contrast, the main subject matter of personal responsibility is one's responsibilities as a person. For example, keeping a promise to a friend is often a matter of personal responsibility because such a duty arises from the friendship. Serving on a jury when called to do so is an example of civic responsibility because such a duty arises from the person's citizenship. None of the other options given accurately describe the main subject matter of civic responsibility. For example, while a journalist might see accurate reporting of government actions as his or her civic responsibility, such reporting is not the main subject matter of civic responsibility and is also a responsibility that arises from that journalist's employment. Similar reasoning applies to a person's responsibilities as a government worker. This eliminates options A and D. Civic responsibility does not primarily concern inter-government relations; this eliminates option B.

71. C: The 26th Amendment is the youth voting rights amendment allowing 18-year-olds to vote, which was ratified under the Nixon administration. The Vietnam War gave more urgency to the "old enough to fight, old enough to vote" slogan. The other amendment choices are in similar time frames and close enough to the 26th Amendment to possibly confuse a student who has not fully studied some of the more important amendments such as the 26th.

72. B: Oligarchy is defined as the rule by few. An example is aristocracy, which in ancient Greece, was government by an elite group of citizens as opposed to a monarchy. In later times, it meant government by the class of aristocrats, a privileged group, as opposed to democracy. The rule of one is called autocracy. Examples include monarchy, dictatorship, and many others. The rule by law is called a republic. Some examples are constitutional republics, parliamentary republics, and federal republics. The rule by many could apply to democracy, which governs according to the people's votes, or to the collective leadership form of socialism, where no one individual has too much power.

73. C: Article III judges are appointed for life and can retire at 65. They can only be removed from their posts by impeachment in the House and conviction in the Senate. Having judges serve life terms is meant to allow them to serve without being governed by the changing opinions of the public.

74. B: The President may veto legislation passed by Congress. The executive branch has this "check" on the legislative branch.

75. A: The citizens usually elect members of the local government such as mayors and city council. However, the state grants local governments their authority. State and local governments work independently and do not share authority the way the federal and state governments share power.

76. B: While all the titles have a connection of some kind to at least one or two items on the given list, choice B provides the best title for the list to show what all the items have in common: reasons for US involvement in the Korean War. The policy of containment is only one element that might fall under the larger subject of reasons for US involvement in the Korean War. The United Nations item would probably not fall under a title about McCarthyism or the HUAC committee, because those were more internal to the US only.

77. A: It is not true that England's defeat of the Spanish Armada in 1588 ended their war with Spain. It did establish England's naval dominance and strengthened England's future colonization of the New World, but the actual war between England and Spain did not end until 1604. It is true that Henry VIII's desire to divorce Catherine of Aragon strengthened English expansionism. Catherine was Spanish, and Henry split from the Catholic Church because it prohibited divorce. Henry's rejection of his Spanish wife and his subsequent support of the Protestant movement angered King Philip II of Spain and destroyed the formerly close ties between the two countries. When Elizabeth became Queen of England, she supported the Reformation as a Protestant, which also contributed to English colonization. Sir Francis Drake, one of the best-known English sea captains during this time period, would attack and plunder Spanish ships that had plundered Native Americans, adding to the enmity between Spain and England. Queen Elizabeth invested in Drake's voyages and gave him her support in claiming territories for England.

78. C: Jonathan Trumbull is the correct answer for which Founding Father was governor of Connecticut during and after the Revolutionary War. The other names are all of Founding Fathers, but none were governors of Connecticut. Rush, Witherspoon and Carroll all signed the Declaration of Independence; Carroll was a US Senator for Maryland, while Rush lived in Pennsylvania and Witherspoon in New Jersey.

79. A: Brown v. Board of Education was decided in 1954. Rosa Parks was arrested in 1955. The lunch counter sit-ins were staged in 1960. The March on Washington took place in 1963.

80. C: The telegraph was a gigantic leap forward in the realm of communications. Before the telegraph, messages could take days, weeks, or months to reach their intended recipient, based upon the distance that they had to travel. The telegraph allowed people to send messages through use of electric signals transmitted over telegraph wires, allowing for instantaneous communications. The main drawbacks to the telegraph included the need to "translate" the message into and out of the appropriate telegraphic code and that the telegraph could only relay one message at a time. In contrast, the telephone allowed for spoken communication between people at different locations, increasing the efficiency and speed as the people on each end of the conversation could communicate multiple messages quickly and in one telephone conversation.

81. D: The Louisiana Purchase actually increased the US's territory by 100% overnight, not 50%. The Louisiana territory doubled the size of the nation. It is true that Jefferson initially sent a delegation to Paris to see if Napoleon would agree to sell only New Orleans to the United States. It is also true that Napoleon, who expected America to encroach on Louisiana, decided to avoid this by offering to sell the entire territory to the US It is likewise true that America only had authority to buy New Orleans. Nevertheless, the delegation accepted Napoleon's offer of all of Louisiana. Due to his belief in strict interpretation of the Constitution, Jefferson did require approval from Congress to make the purchase. When his advisors characterized the purchase as being within his purview based on the presidential power to make treaties, Congress agreed.

82. D: Political corruption was not an immediate effect of the rapid urban growth during this time. The accelerated growth of cities in America did soon result in services being unable to keep up with that growth. The results of this included deficiencies in clean water delivery and garbage collection, causing poor sanitation. That poor sanitation led to outbreaks of cholera and typhus, as well as typhoid fever epidemics. Police and fire fighting services could not keep up with the population increases, and were often inadequate. With people moving to the cities at such a fast rate, there were also deficits in housing and public transportation.

83. A: The latest occurring decolonization event was the Eastern Bloc and Soviet Satellite states of Armenia, Azerbaijan, Estonia, Georgia, Kazakhstan, Kyrgyzstan, Latvia, Lithuania, Moldova, Russia, Tajikistan, Turkmenistan, Ukraine, and Uzbekistan, which all became independent from the Soviet Union in 1991. (Note: This was the last decolonization of the Cold War years, as the end of the Soviet Union marked the end of the Cold War.) Canada completed its independence from British Parliament via the Canada Act in 1982. In the Caribbean, the Bahamas gained independence from the United Kingdom in 1973. Algeria won its independence from France when the Algerian War of Independence, begun in 1954, ended in 1962.

84. D: Because the Puritans took on a Reformed theology, they were in this sense Calvinists. However, many Puritans endorsed radical views that criticized such Calvinists as John (Jean) Calvin and Huldrych (Ulrich) Zwingli in Switzerland. Not only were Puritans critical of Calvinists despite their mutual Reformed approaches, reciprocally many Calvinists were opposed to the Puritans as well. The Puritan movement changed less in American colonies than in England during the 1660s. Following the Restoration (1660) and the Uniformity Act (1662) in England, nearly all of the Puritan clergy objected and left the Church of England, thereby creating a dramatic change in the movement in that country. Nevertheless, in America, the Puritans who had emigrated from England continued their original Puritan traditions for a longer time, as they had neither the same Anglican Church as in England nor the legislation restoring earlier church status against which the English Puritans had reacted.

85. C: The speech was given in 1972 by President Richard M. Nixon, who was about to become the first US president to visit the People's Republic of China. The other presidents listed are good guesses, as they are from similar time periods and might have made similar speeches about China and the Soviet Union, but they are incorrect choices.

86. D: In point 14 of his 1918 speech, Wilson proposed a League of Nations, which would serve as a precursor to the United Nations. Having the US involved in such a league was a contrast to Wilson's pre-war policy of neutrality. The other choices make references to phrases found in the excerpt, but they are not statements that contrast with a policy of neutrality and are incorrect answer choices.

87. D: All the laws (D) named were instrumental in spurring westward migration to the Great Plains. The Homestead Act (A), passed in 1862, gave settlers 160 acres of land at no monetary cost in exchange for a commitment to cultivating the land for five years. The Timber Culture Act (B), passed in 1873, gave the settlers 160 acres more of land in exchange for planting trees on one quarter of the acreage. The Desert Land Act (C), passed in 1877, allowed buyers who would irrigate the land to buy 640 acres for only 25 cents an acre. Thus, (D), all of these laws were instrumental in spurring westward migration to the Great Plains during that period, is correct.

88. C: A primary source is a first-hand account that is written by someone directly involved in the event being described. Sources like Wikipedia or a colleague's lecture notes would be considered either secondary or tertiary sources. While a newspaper article by an analyst written weeks following the massacre might cite primary sources (like the interviews from the soldiers who were in the massacre), it is not itself a primary source.

89. C: Primary sources are sources that were created at the time of the event in question. For examples, recordings of Martin Luther King's speeches, newspaper accounts of King's activities at the time of those activities, and King's written documents are all primary resources regarding Martin Luther King's work. Secondary sources, such as a history book that contains a subchapter on the work of MLK, are secondhand and are almost always created after the fact. This eliminates choice A. Secondary sources do not need to be text-only, nor visual only, as the example above illustrates; this eliminates both options B and D.

90. B: Amorosa writes about her family and about her anticipation of the *Quinceañera,* a traditional birthday celebration in Latin cultures. She describes her family members in detail, as well as that she is involved in soccer, school and art classes. Amorosa is a typical student in her interests and identification as part of a family unit. She clearly also identifies herself within her cultural heritage through her discussion of the *Quinceañera.* This is a celebration with a long history and specific customs that are shared by *Latina* girls and women, even within the United States.

91. B: Students are more motivated to inquire and learn new things when the topic at hand is relevant to their real lives. Since Amorosa is obviously looking forward to her *Quinceañera,* she may enjoy researching similar celebrations and customs inherent in other cultures. By relating this cultural research to an event, she is anticipating, her teacher will help her identify relevant similarities across many cultures. Amorosa will also have an opportunity to practice understanding contrasts between various events as well as cultures throughout the project that will aid her in deepening cultural awareness in the future.

92. C: One reason for laws and rules that we can communicate to young children to help them understand important civics concepts is that they confer greater predictability, order, and security to our society and hence our lives. Another reason is that laws and rules identify for citizens which behaviors are acceptable and which are unacceptable, rather than only punishing the latter (A). Another reason is that laws and rules delegate various responsibilities to citizens, rather than interfering with these (B). An additional reason is that laws and rules *limit* the power of persons in authority positions to prevent them from abusing their positions, rather than increasing that power (D).

93. C: A key to the question is the relation between supply and demand. The use of graphics in presentation software can be used effectively to show supply and demand curves, which effectively show the relation between supply and demand. Neither options A and B explain the relation between supply and demand; option A merely involves listing such terms, and B merely involves understanding the terms in isolation, but not the relation between them. Option D can be rejected because it concerns only demand, not supply and demand.

94. B: Developing students' awareness of major themes related to social studies in the early childhood classroom requires that teachers implement activities to first demonstrate where these themes occur in daily life. Doing so places learning in a familiar, relevant context for young children and establishes the foundation necessary for applying these concepts to a larger scale. Cultural awareness refers to one's understanding of differences in beliefs, traditions, values, and experiences among individuals from other groups, and it is necessary for functioning as a productive member of society. Fostering this skill in the classroom promotes students' ability to communicate respectfully, collaborate with a diverse range of individuals, and build upon their own knowledge by learning to appreciate the perspectives of others. In this example activity, the teacher fosters students' ability to recognize that their background may differ from that of other individuals in the class, thus building a fundamental awareness of their own and others' cultures.

95. A: In *Dred Scott v Sandford*, the slave Dred Scott attempted to gain his freedom based upon the fact that he had lived with his owners in abolitionist states during his lifetime. The Supreme Court denied his claim, stating that he was not a citizen of the United States and therefore could not bring suit in a federal court. This case illustrates the fact that this nation has been debating the concept of citizenship, and who can become a citizen, for centuries. Students will find their understanding of current events deepened by historical knowledge of laws and social belief systems.

Science

96. C: Sources of renewable energy include geothermal power, solar energy, and wind power. Sources of nonrenewable energy include nuclear power and fossil fuels like coal, natural gas, and crude oil.

97. C: A laccolith is formed when an intrusion of magma injected between two layers of sedimentary rock forces the overlying strata upward to create a dome-like form. Eventually, the magma cools, the sedimentary rock wears away and the formation is exposed. Sills and dikes are both examples of sheet intrusions, where magma has inserted itself into other rock. Sills are horizontal and dikes are vertical. A caldera is a crater-like feature that was formed from the collapse of a volcano after erupting.

98. B: When an astronomer observing stars detects a blue shift, he can conclude the star is moving closer or toward him. This is an example of the practical application of the Doppler effect in astronomy as applied to electromagnetic waves. The Doppler effect explains the change of wavelength caused by motion of the source or the relative difference in velocity between the observer and the source. When observing stars, a red shift or blue shift can be used to measure the speed that stars and galaxies are approaching or receding. Blue light has a higher frequency than red light. A red shift indicates a receding source.

99. D: Sources of renewable energy include geothermal power, solar energy, and wind power. Sources of nonrenewable energy include nuclear power and fossil fuels like coal, natural gas, and crude oil.

100. D: Of these options, the only real direct impact of climate change is the rising sea level. This is due to the melting glaciers and ice sheets. Also, the oceans expand slightly as they get warmer.

101. B: Sedimentary rocks are formed in layers on the surface of the Earth when the results of erosion and other processes deposit sediment. Some sedimentary rock remains loose; some is cemented together by chemicals, minerals, or electrical attraction. Igneous rock (C) is formed when volcanoes erupt, spewing lava onto the Earth's surface where it cools and hardens into rock. Metamorphic rock is formed when igneous and sedimentary rocks deeply buried in the crust of the Earth are subjected to extreme heat and/or pressure. These forces change, i.e., metamorphose, the structure of the rocks, creating metamorphic rock. Therefore, (D) is incorrect.

102. C: Tropical climate zones are characterized by frequent rainfall, especially during the monsoon season, and by moderate temperatures that vary little from season to season or between night and day. Tropical zones do experience frequent rainfall, which leads to abundant vegetation.

103. A: Water actually has its lowest volume at four degrees Celsius. Water stops contracting at four degrees Celsius. Water expands as it cools from four degrees Celsius to zero degrees Celsius.

104. B: When land cools off rapidly at night and the ocean water stays relatively warm, it creates a land breeze. Sea breeze, or onshore breeze, occurs when the land heats the air above it. This heated, warmer air is less dense and rises. The cooler air from above the sea and higher sea level pressure creates a wind flow in the direction of the land. Coastal areas often have these cooler breezes. A monsoon is a seasonal wind in southern Asia that blows southwest in one season and northeast in another. The southwest winds in the summer bring heavy rain. The trade winds are the steady easterlies about the equator.

105. A: The body's main fuel is the simple sugar glucose. Complex carbohydrates provide the body with sustained energy by slowly breaking down into glucose.

106. C: The fraction of offspring that that have the genotype BbSs is $\frac{4}{16}$. A dihybrid cross considers two traits at a time, in this case, eye color and hair color. In the parent (P) generation, a parent with the genotype BBSS would be crossed with a parent with the genotype bbss. The offspring are considered the F1 generation and all would have the genotype BbSs. This question asks about the F2 generation, which is the offspring between a cross of the F1 generation. Therefore, the parent genotypes in this question would be BbSs. To solve, develop a Punnet square of 16 cells. Each parent will produce the following gametes: BS, Bs, bS, bs. Place these across the top and the side. After completing the square, the resulting offspring show that four would have the genotype BbSs.

P → F1

	BS
bs	BbSs

F1 → F2

	BS	**Bs**	**bS**	**bs**
BS	BBSS	BBSs	BbSS	BbSs
Bs	BBSs	BBss	BbSs	Bbss
bS	BbSS	BbSs	bbSS	bbSs
bs	BbSs	Bbss	bbSs	bbss

107. C: Genes code for proteins, and genes are discrete lengths of DNA on chromosomes. An allele is a variant of a gene (different DNA sequence). In diploid organisms, there may be two versions of each gene.

108. B: Stomata are the pores of the plant that open to release water via transpiration or close during adverse conditions like a drought to prevent the plant from dehydration. Stomata are flanked by guard cells that can respond to stimuli and regulate opening and closing. Pith refers to the central, spongy part of the stem in vascular plants. Sepals are modified leave that protect the flower bud before it opens.

109. B: Water can stabilize the temperature of living things because of its high specific heat capacity, which means that it takes a while to heat or cool. This ability to minimize changes in temperature protects the body from sudden temperature shifts that could disrupt normal physiological processes. While water does help decrease body temperature through evaporation, this is not a comprehensive description of water's overall role in temperature regulation.

110. D: The circulatory system and gas exchange with the environment is not paired correctly. It is the respiratory system that exchanges gases with the environment by delivering oxygen to the bloodstream and releasing carbon dioxide. The circulatory system transports nutrients, gases, hormones, and blood to and away from cells. The muscle system controls movement through three types of muscle tissue. The nervous system controls sensory responses by carrying impulses away from and toward the cell body. The digestive system breaks down food for absorption into the bloodstream where it is delivered to cells for respiration.

111. C: Plants reproduce both asexually and sexually. Asexual reproduction occurs through runners that some plants extend to root new growth, through plant cuttings being rooted in water and then planted, and through grafts. Plants reproduce sexually through fertilization, wherein plant gametes combine, contributing chromosomes from both sides, similarly to how animals mate. The other answer options are correct.

112. D: Human beings, like other mammals, birds, fish, reptiles, and spiders, have simple life cycles in that they are either born live or hatched from eggs, and then grow to adulthood. Frogs (A), newts (B), and grasshoppers (C) undergo metamorphoses wherein their forms change. Frogs and newts are amphibians; they begin life underwater, breathing through gills, but breathe through lungs by adulthood and move from the water to live on the land. Grasshoppers hatch from eggs into larvae, wormlike juvenile forms that do most of the feeding they need; then they progress to adulthood.

113. C: All typical living organisms need food, water, sunlight, and air. Shelter, space, and nurturing are essential for most organisms, but they are technically indirect needs that are not crucial to sustaining life.

114. B: Glycogen is a polysaccharide, a molecule composed of many bonded glucose molecules. Glucose is a carbohydrate, and all carbohydrates are composed of only carbon, oxygen, and hydrogen. Most other metabolic compounds contain other atoms, particularly nitrogen, phosphorus, and sulfur.

115. C: In general, atomic radius increases moving down a group due to the increasing number of electron shells. In general, atomic radius decreases moving from left to right across a period due to the increasing number of protons in the energy level; therefore, atoms of elements in the bottom-left corner of the periodic table tend to have the largest atomic radii.

116. B: Anabolic processes are those that use energy to build larger molecules. In cells, adenosine triphosphate (ATP) is used as a source of energy. A condensation reaction joins two molecules together to make a larger molecule and, in the process, also produces a water molecule. Condensation reactions are important in protein synthesis. Anabolic processes are often reduction reactions. Catabolism breaks down molecules and usually generates energy. Catabolic reactions are often oxidation reactions. Hydrolysis is a catabolic process where water is added to a molecule and then split, resulting in the molecule breaking apart into two different molecules. Hydrolysis is the opposite of condensation.

117. B: Work is defined as the force used to move a mass over a distance. The amount of energy used to accomplish a job is a non-scientific definition of work. The amount of energy used per unit of time is the definition of power. Energy stored in an object due to its position is the definition of potential energy.

118. B: The phenomenon known as weightlessness is caused by an object being in free fall. An object in space still experiences a gravitational force due to the earth, but if that object is in orbit, it's effectively free falling around the earth, which causes it to experience weightlessness. Here, proposition I is wrong because you have to be pretty far away from a star for gravity to become negligible. In fact, objects only stay in orbit because the earth's gravity pulls on them and causes them to change direction. This means the usual experience of weight is lost, as you can see by the floating objects and people inside an orbiting spaceship. The same thing happens to a ski jumper, who is in free fall after he or she jumps. If the jumper is carrying a rock, for example, that rock will feel weightless while the jumper is in the air. A rolled baseball is not in freefall and does not experience weightlessness.

119. A: In a scientific experiment, the dependent variable is the condition that is being tested and measured. The independent variable is the condition that is being changed or controlled. In this example, the amount of salt is varied, and the boiling point of water is measured. Therefore, the independent variable is the amount of salt, and the dependent variable is the temperature at which the water boils.

120. C: As the ring spins, the wall of the ring exerts centripetal force on your body. This force also causes friction between your back and the wall, and that's why you don't fall when the floor is removed, assuming the frictional force is large enough to overcome gravity. As the speed of rotation increases, the force exerted by the wall on your body increases, so the frictional force between you and the wall increases. Answer B is factually correct, but it does not explain why you do not fall—centripetal force does cause you to change direction. Also note that "centrifugal force" is an illusion; because you feel the wall pushing against your back, you feel like you're being pushed outwards. In fact, you're being pulled inwards, but the wall is also being pulled inwards and is pushing against you. Finally, choice D is incorrect because you are not weightless on a ride like this.

121. B: Solubility is the amount of solute present in saturated solution. For a gas solute in a liquid solvent, increasing the temperature increases the kinetic energy of the gas molecules, which decreases the solubility of the gas in the liquid. Increasing the pressure of the gas increases the number of particles escaping from the surface and increases the solubility. For a solid solute in a liquid solvent, increasing the temperature increases the kinetic energy, which increases the number of collisions and increases the solubility. Increasing the pressure of a solid solute in a liquid has little or no effect on solubility.

122. C: The greater the mass of an object, the greater the force necessary to move it. A shot put has greater mass than a tennis ball; therefore, more force is required to throw it a certain distance than is required to a throw a tennis ball the same distance. Conversely, less force is required to throw the tennis ball that distance than the shot put. Remember, both the tennis ball and the shot put are governed by the principle of inertia, meaning that force must be applied to both to set them in motion. Potential energy does not explain the difference in necessary force; neither is it clear that the tennis ball has more potential energy. Typically, to throw both the tennis ball and the shot put, one would throw them horizontally; this doesn't explain the difference in necessary force.

123. C: Catalysts lower the energy barrier between products and reactants and thus increase the reaction rate. Catalysts do not change the thermodynamic position of equilibrium, reaction temperature, or product purity on their own.

124. D: Exhaust fumes are an ever-present concern, while the others are incidents that might or might not occur. A combustion engine of any kind produces fumes which can rapidly cause health damage, brain damage, or death if allowed to fill an inadequately ventilated space. Therefore, activities of this kind are usually conducted near an open garage door or loading dock if not out-of-doors. A situation guaranteed to happen—the production of fumes—is of higher priority than incidental dangers.

125. C: When performing a dissection in class, decaying specimens can be permitted under certain circumstances, but unknown specimens are never permitted. Rinsing the specimen before handling can help wash away excess preservative, which may be irritating. Disposing of harmful chemicals according to district regulations is always required. Excusing students with open sores on their hands that cannot be covered is a good precaution. Exposure to pathogens and toxic chemicals can occur through open breaks in the skin.

126. B: Acids and bases will react violently if accidentally mixed, as will reducing and oxidizing agents. Both reactions can be highly exothermic and uncontrollable.

127. B: The activity described uses each of these skills. The children use scientific observation to note what happens when they try the different ball-ramp actions the teacher suggests (and think of themselves), and they discuss their findings with and report them to one another and the teacher (A). They use inference when they realize similarities, differences, and patterns among the different actions and what these mean, and they use prediction to answer the teacher's questions about "what would happen if..." before testing them by performing the suggested actions (C). They use measurement when observing the height and length of the ramps, the speed at which the balls roll down them, the distance they roll, and when counting the numbers of balls and ramps. And they use comparison (D) when they find the differences in the effects on speed and distance of varying ramp sizes, ramp numbers, ball numbers, etc.

128. B: Teachers and students should always wear goggles and aprons or lab coats when working with chemicals, including cleanup. Gloves should be worn as needed.

129. B: A properly adjusted flame should be nearly colorless or blue with an inner and outer cone. If the flame is yellow, increase the air supply. If the flame burns noisily, reduce the gas supply.

130. A: Young children are naturally curious about the environment. They typically ask many questions and enjoy finding out new things; these represent natural inquiry and discovery. Hence activities involving scientific inquiry and discovery are appealing to them. Young children need not be taught to question and explore (B) as they want to do these naturally; they need only to be guided by teachers in their questioning and exploration to discover scientific ideas and principles. Because very young children see the world as revolving around themselves and are most interested in activities where they are central, teachers should design activities for them that focus not outside the self (C) but focus on the children themselves. For example, when building skeletons out of dry pasta or other common household materials, teachers can have children use photos of their faces for heads. Teachers can use many pre-existing activities in preschool for discovering science, including cooking and art (D)—e.g., water solubility of substances, mixing paint colors, etc.

131. C: When building block structures and then dismantling them, children learn concepts of part-whole relations. They learn concepts of shape (A) when they realize that some objects roll away from them and others do not. They learn concepts of weight (B) when they try to lift different objects and find some are heavier and some lighter. As babies, they quickly learn concepts of temporal sequences (D) when they awaken wet and/or hungry and then their parents change and/or feed them. As toddlers, they also learn temporal concepts through playing, tiring, and sleeping.

132. D: Providing young children with opportunities to self-assess as they participate in scientific inquiry is beneficial in fostering continuous learning and development. Doing so allows students to take ownership over their learning, thus increasing overall engagement and encouraging further scientific exploration. Self-assessment practices prompt students to monitor their own progress, identify personal strengths and areas for improvement, and recognize the need for support. Incorporating color-coded cards into learning activities for students to communicate their level of understanding is a highly effective self-assessment technique. This strategy requires students to continuously evaluate their own performances as they engage in scientific investigation and determine the need for additional assistance to be successful in achieving learning targets.

133. A: This is an issue that would be regulated by the Food and Drug Administration (FDA), as it regulates the packaging of meat products, among many other types of food. Answer B would not be an issue for the FDA. The Environmental Protection Agency (EPA) regulates issues regarding the environment as well as Superfund cleanups. Neither answer C, about genetic engineering of humans, nor answer D, about cell use in industry, relate to food and drugs and would not fall under the jurisdiction of the FDA.

134. D: A good hypothesis must be testable. This means it may be proved or disproved by testing using a controlled experiment. A controlled experiment may have several constants but only one independent variable.

135. A: X-rays were put to clinical use within a month of their discovery to image bone fractures and foreign objects in the body. Later, they were used to locate tumors and to fight cancer. Distant galaxies have been discovered by the detection of X-rays from stars. X-rays are commonly used as security scanners.

136. B: While land reclamation destroys nearby habitats, it doesn't increase biodiversity. The destruction of habitats leads to a decrease in biodiversity.

137. B: When sulfur dioxide and nitrogen dioxide mix with water and other substances in the atmosphere, they produce sulfuric acid and nitric acid. These acids kill plants and animals when they reach the surface of the earth.

138. C: In order to have accurate measurements, the use of a graduated cylinder would be best. A triple beam balance measures the mass of an object in grams. A flask and a test tube are used to contain a liquid while being heated or stored.

139. D: Although data from previous trials is important for the final lab report and results summary, it is not important for the current trial being tested. A final summary will incorporate all trial data results and observations in order to determine a final conclusion about the results. Temperature, color changes, and the production of a gas or odor indicate that a chemical change has occurred and should be recorded as an observation.

140. A: The control in an experiment is not subject to the variable being tested—in this case, the new drug. The volunteers who are given the drug comprise the experimental group.

Mathematics

141. C: When you have a ratio, you can find the fraction that each part of the ratio is of the whole by dividing a part by the sum of the parts. Since the ratio of wages and benefits to other costs is 2: 3, the amount of money spent on wages and benefits is $\frac{2}{2+3} = \frac{2}{5}$ of total operational costs.

$$\frac{2}{5} \times \$130{,}000 = \$52{,}000$$

142. A: The inequality will be less than or equal to, since he may spend $100 or less on his purchase.

143. C: The slope of a line can be found using any two points and the formula slope $= \frac{y_2-y_1}{x_2-x_1}$. The only points that give a slope of $-\frac{2}{3}$ are $(-3,-1)$, $(-6,1)$, and $(0,-3)$.

$$\frac{1-(-1)}{-6-(-3)} = \frac{2}{-3} = -\frac{2}{3}$$

$$\frac{-3-1}{0-(-6)} = \frac{-4}{6} = -\frac{2}{3}$$

144. A: Marcus needs $325 for the new gaming system. If he earns $6.50 an hour, the number of hours he needs to work can be determined by dividing $325 by $6.50 which is written as $\frac{325}{6.50} = x$. Multiplying both sides of the equation by 6.50 yields $6.50x = 325$.

145. D: The constant of proportionality is equal to the slope. Using the points, $(2, -8)$ and $(5, -20)$, the slope may be written as $\frac{-20-(-8)}{5-2}$, which equals -4.

146. D: To determine the smallest volume, it is simplest to calculate the volume of each and then compare:

Solid	Volume Formula	Result
Cube	$V = s^3$	$(5\text{ cm})^3 = 125\text{ cm}^3$
Rectangular Prism	$V = l \times w \times h$	$(5\text{ cm})(3\text{ cm})(7\text{ cm}) = 105\text{ cm}^3$
Cylinder	$V = \pi \times r^2 \times h$	$\pi(3\text{ cm})^2(4\text{ cm}) \approx 113.1\text{ cm}^3$
Cone	$V = \frac{1}{3}(\pi \times r^2 \times h)$	$\frac{1}{3}\pi(3\text{ cm})^2(10\text{ cm}) \approx 94.2\text{ cm}^3$

From this it is clear that the cone has the smallest volume.

147. B: A regular solid prism is a solid, three-dimensional shape which has length, width, and height. The bases are of the same shape, and the shape of the other faces depend on the shape of the bases. The volume of a regular solid prism can be determined by multiplying the area of the base by the height of the prism.

148. C: The following equation may be written and solved for x: $\sin 40° = \frac{x}{6}$. Multiplying both sides of the equation by 6 gives: $6 \cdot \sin 40° = x$, or $x \approx 3.9$.

149. D: The Pythagorean theorem may be used to find the diagonal distance from the top of his head to the base of the shadow. Using the following equation, we can determine this distance, c: $5.8^2 + 6.2^2 = c^2$. Thus, $c \approx 8.5$. The distance is approximately 8.5 ft.

150. C: The original triangle was reflected across the x-axis. When reflecting across the x-axis, the x-values of each point remain the same, but the y-values of the points will be opposites.

$$(1,4) \to (1,-4) \quad (5,4) \to (5,-4) \quad (3,8) \to (3,-8)$$

151. D: The decimal point is 4 places to the right of the first digit, 4. Thus, $47{,}800 = 4.78 \times 10^4$.

152. B: The additive inverse property states that the sum of a number and its negative value is 0.

153. D: The commutative property of multiplication states that the order in which two numbers are multiplied does not matter: $a \times b = b \times a$.

154. C: The set of integers is contained within the set of rational numbers and is therefore a subset of the rational numbers. A rational number may be written as the ratio, $\frac{a}{b}$, where a and b are integers and $b \neq 0$.

155. B: The population is approximately 36,000, so one-quarter of the population consists of about 9,000 individuals under age 35. A third of 9,000 is 3,000, which is the approximate number of students in grades K–12. Since there are thirteen grades, divide 3,000 by 13. There are about 230 students in each grade. So, the number of fourth graders is between 200 and 300.

156. D: Follow the order of operations, which in this case is simply left to right with multiplication and division. $\frac{5}{6} \times \frac{7}{3} \times \frac{5}{9} = \frac{35}{18} \times \frac{5}{9} = \frac{175}{162}$.

157. D: The 5 is in the tenths place, the 9 in the hundredths place, and the 3 in the thousandths place. Thus, 0.593 is equal to the sum of the product of 5 and $\frac{1}{10}$, the product of 9 and $\frac{1}{100}$, and the product of 3 and $\frac{1}{1{,}000}$.

158. C: The amount he saves is equal to $0.1 \times \$2{,}450$. Thus, he saves \$245.

159. D: The percent change can be found using the following formula.

$$\%\text{ Change} = \frac{\text{new} - \text{old}}{\text{old}} \times 100$$

The old value is his current rent (750), and the new value is his new monthly rent (900).

$$\%\text{ Change} = \frac{900 - 750}{750} \times 100$$
$$\%\text{ Change} = \frac{150}{750} \times 100$$
$$\%\text{ Change} = \frac{1}{5} \times 100$$
$$\%\text{ Change} = 20$$

Since the percent change is positive, this represents a percent increase of 20%.

160. C: Apply the order of operations.

$16 \div (6-4)^2 = 64$	$8 - 2(7-4) = 18$	$2^3 \div 2 - 2(2) = 0$	$2 + 3(2^2) = 20$
$16 \div 2^2 = 64$	$8 - 2(3) = 18$	$8 \div 2 - 2(2) = 0$	$2 + 3(4) = 20$
$16 \div 4 = 64$	$8 - 6 = 18$	$4 - 4 = 0$	$2 + 12 = 20$
$4 \neq 64$	$2 \neq 18$	$0 = 0$	$14 \neq 20$

161. A: The probability of the mutually exclusive events A or B occurring may be written as $P(A \text{ or } B) = P(A) + P(B)$. The probability of obtaining a number greater than 5 is $\frac{3}{8}$ because 3 of the 8 sections are greater than 5: 6, 7, and 8. The probability of obtaining a 2 is $\frac{1}{8}$ because this refers to 1 of the 8 sections. Thus, $P(A \text{ or } B) = \frac{3}{8} + \frac{1}{8} = \frac{4}{8} = \frac{1}{2}$.

162. A: A correlation of 0.9 is a strong correlation because it is close to 1. Recall that the closer a correlation coefficient is to −1 or 1, the stronger the correlation. A correlation of −1 or 1 is perfect.

163. B: Correlation coefficients range from −1 to 1, with values close to −1 or 1 representing strong relationships. Thus, a correlation coefficient of 0.2 represents a weak correlation because it is close to 0 rather than 1.

164. A: A six-sided die has an equal number of odd and even numbers on the six faces. The probability that an odd number will appear when the die is rolled is equal to the probability that an even number will appear, or 0.5. The eight-sided die also has an equal number of odd and even numbers on its eight faces. The probability that an odd number will appear when the die is rolled is therefore also equal to the probability that an even umber will appear, or 0.5.

165. B: The probability may be written as $P(E \text{ and } H) = P(E) \times P(H)$. The probability of rolling an even number on a die is $E = \frac{3}{6} = \frac{1}{2}$. The probability of a coin landing on heads is $H = \frac{1}{2}$. Substituting the probability of each event gives $P(E \text{ and } H) = \frac{1}{2} \times \frac{1}{2} = \frac{1}{4}$.

166. A: It is possible for teachers to use effective manipulative objects to instruct young children in early math concepts by purchasing, constructing, and finding them. Geometric shapes, linking cubes, magnetized numbers and boards; weights and scales; math games and blocks; tangrams; color tiles; flash cards; play money and working toy cash registers, etc., can be bought from stores, catalogs, and online. Teachers can also construct useful math manipulatives from everyday materials, and they can use found objects without further assembly, like pebbles, seashells, buttons, bottle caps, keys, cardboard tubes, coffee stirrers, etc. It is not true that either buying (B) or making (C) manipulatives is superior; teachers can do one, the other, or both depending on budgets, time, availability, and preference. Young children learn best when ideas are embodied in concrete physical objects they can look at, touch, and handle, rather than when ideas are presented to them abstractly (D).

167. C: Normally developing young children typically learn to count before they have learned the names of all of the numbers. They do NOT typically learn all number names before learning to count (A). They do NOT typically acquire both skills at the same time (B). And they do NOT typically vary individually in the order (D) of acquiring these skills.

168. C: Addition and subtraction of whole numbers up to 20 using concrete and pictorial models and number sentences is the appropriate level for first-grade students. Numbers up to 1,000 and number pairs are appropriate for third-grade students. Counting by ones and tens is appropriate for kindergarten.

169. D: Being aware that patterns (regular repetitions) and relationships (associations between/among things) exist in the world affords us greater self-efficacy about our interacting with the environment, as well as increases our sense of confidence in the environment itself (C). This awareness not only helps us to understand sequences of events; it moreover enables us to predict the next event in the series before it occurs (B). Having an awareness of patterns and relationships in things also informs our understanding of the basic structure of those things (A).

170. D: Real numbers include all rational and irrational numbers. Rational numbers include all integers. The set of real numbers include the other three sets.

171. D: Number lines can help students understand the concepts of positive and negative numbers. Fraction strips are most commonly used with fractions. Venn diagrams are commonly used when comparing groups. Shaded regions are commonly used with fractions or percentages.

172. A: It is true that manipulative objects have been found so effective for young children's learning that Horizons and other early math curricula actually require their use. Manipulatives that children can see, feel, and work with not only help young children who learn best through visual, tactile, and kinesthetic modalities, but they also help other young children (B) because young children's learning is mainly via looking at, touching, holding, arranging, and moving concrete things as well as being fun (D). Young children mostly do not understand abstract concepts yet, and they are even less likely to understand them when presented in abstract form, but they are more able to access some abstract ideas that are presented in concrete forms (C).

173. C: Adults can help young children understand the concepts that time passes and is counted and measured by engaging them in counting activities, getting them used to counting in general, telling them how much time various activities took, and showing them the second hand on a clock or watch and counting "One second, two seconds, three...." Young children typically have NOT yet developed understanding of the abstract concept of time (A). However, adults *should* refer to time periods with young children, even before they understand these (B). For example, they can tell children, "You may play for five more minutes before bedtime." Making such references will aid young children's eventual realization of the passage of time. But young children will typically *not* understand such abstract concepts as yesterday/today/tomorrow (D); adults can use more concrete referents, e.g., "after supper" or "before bedtime" until children are older.

174. A: When the teacher supplies the student with the formal math vocabulary word "classifying", s/he is emphasizing the connection of the child's informal math activity of sorting rocks with the formal math vocabulary word that describes it. Asking the child how s/he is sorting the rocks (B) is a better example of the teacher's emphasizing math communication than vocabulary (by having the child explain). Asking, after the child finishes sorting rocks, what other ways s/he could sort them (C) is a better example of emphasizing problem-solving skills than math vocabulary. Therefore (D) is incorrect.

175. D: One-to-one correspondence refers to students' ability to individually count items within a set with the understanding that each item can only be counted one time. Development of this early numeracy concept is essential to building a range of foundational mathematical skills; therefore it must be addressed explicitly when a student is experiencing difficulty. Formatively observing students as they work allows teachers to evaluate overall understanding and recognize when an individual is struggling so that they can implement the appropriate supports. Counting mats provide a multisensory approach to mathematical learning and can be differentiated to support students' understanding of a variety of skills, including one-to-one correspondence. Teachers can utilize this resource to have students physically move manipulatives as they count upward to represent a numerical value while simultaneously visualizing its quantity, thus strengthening their understanding of the concept.

Practice Test #2

Language Arts and Reading

1. Which of the following is most accurate about the relationship between the physics of thinking and speaking as these inform classroom instruction in listening actively?

a. Because thinking outpaces speech, students' minds wander, so listening is less effective than reading.
b. The disparity between speaking and thinking speeds is conducive to active listening via summarizing.
c. The process of listening is an inherently social interaction; the process of learning is not equally social.
d. The process of learning is essentially a reciprocal one, but the process of listening is not as reciprocal.

2. A teacher wants to work on her students' listening comprehension in addition to their reading comprehension since she understands that the skills are interrelated. She has a series of short stories that she thinks the students will enjoy. Which of the following would be the best supplement to typical written comprehension exercises?

a. Preview the content and then read the stories aloud to the students. Assess listening comprehension through verbal and written questions.
b. Ask the students to choose one story each to read aloud to a small group. Encourage the students to discuss what they have learned afterward.
c. Assign each student a story to read and require them to write a report on it. Each student should then present his or her report based on what he or she has learned to the class.
d. Have the students read stories aloud to the class, and create mock tests based upon the main ideas which they identify.

3. According to MLA guidelines for writing research papers, which of the following is correct regarding citations of sources found on the internet if the author's name cannot be found quickly on the source page or site?

a. Assume the author is not named, as this is a common occurrence on the internet.
b. Name an agency or corporation as the author if it is the publisher of the source.
c. Author names are often on websites, but sometimes they are hard to find.
d. It is not permissible to cite the book or article title in lieu of an author's name.

4. If a student is writing a thesis on brain disorders, the best source of information would be a(n):

a. medical journals.
b. encyclopedia.
c. webpage.
d. newspaper.

5. Which of the following statements is correct regarding effective speech delivery?

a. Speakers should avoid practicing speeches to appear spontaneous.
b. Verbal and nonverbal communication should seem equally natural.
c. Speakers should avoid using humor because it will distract the audience.
d. Random movements can help sustain the attention of the audience.

6. Of the following attributes of mobile and text media for presenting ideas in public communications, which is a disadvantage?

a. Popularity
b. Timeliness
c. Interactivity
d. Limited length

7. Which of the following is an example of a bandwagon method of appeal?

a. A car is advertised with a beautiful model sitting in it.
b. A soap ad shows someone bathing under a waterfall.
c. An ad sings, "Wouldn't you like to be a pepper, too?"
d. A brand made in USA is shown with an American flag.

8. A student is taking a reading test. The teacher has blocked out a number of words. Each blank is assigned a set of three possible words. The student must select the correct word from each set so that the text makes sense. The student is taking:

a. A cloze test
b. A maze test
c. A multiple-choice quiz
d. A vocabulary test

9. Which of the following is true about the 3N (Notice, Nudge, Narrate) instructional strategy for developing early childhood literacy?

a. It does not incorporate any informal assessment of literacy levels.
b. It uses scaffolding to promote further literacy skills development.
c. It is a strategy that does not integrate any reflective components.
d. This strategy is not found adaptable to games for young children.

10. A third-grade teacher has several students reading above grade level. Most of the remaining students are reading at grade level. There are also a few students reading below grade level. She decides to experiment. Her hypothesis is that by giving the entire class a chapter book above grade level, high-level readers will be satisfied, grade-level readers will be challenged in a positive way, and students reading below grade level will be inspired to improve. Her method is most likely to:

a. Succeed, producing students reading at an Instructional reading level. High-level readers will be happy to be given material appropriate to their reading level. Grade-level readers will challenge themselves to improve reading strategies in order to master the text. Because only a few of the students are reading below grade level, the other students, who feel happy and energized, will inspire the slower readers by modeling success.
b. Succeed, producing students reading at an Independent reading level. High-level readers will independently help grade-level readers who will, in turn, independently help those below grade level.
c. Fail, producing students at a Frustration reading level. Those reading below grade level are likely to give up entirely. Those reading at grade level are likely to get frustrated and form habits that will actually slow down their development.
d. Fail, producing students reading at a Chaotic reading level. By nature, children are highly competitive. The teacher has not taken into consideration multiple learning styles. The children who are at grade level will either become bitter and angry at those whose reading level is above grade level or simply give up. The children reading below grade level will not be able to keep up and will in all likelihood act out their frustration or completely shut down.

11. What have studies found about how teachers interpret and apply research to reading instruction challenges?

a. Teachers make data-based instructional decisions better individually than in small groups.
b. Teachers are generally better at data comprehension than data location in graphs or tables.
c. Teachers do far better at interpreting relationships among variables than question-posing.
d. Teachers plan differentiated instruction better with real (not hypothetical) student scores.

12. How can teachers use portfolio assessments to evaluate student writing?

a. As formative assessments
b. As summative assessments
c. As both formative and summative assessments
d. As neither formative nor summative assessments

13. For which of the following purposes would a teacher use a formative assessment?

a. To get data to inform a school improvement plan
b. To get or keep government funding for the school
c. To get data about individual student performance
d. To get data on student progress over a school year

14. Which of the following choices would be the least effective example of an integrated curriculum that includes language arts instruction?

a. Ms. Smith, a language teacher, confers with Mr. Langston, a history and social studies teacher. Ms. Smith shows Mr. Langston how to model previewing and predicting skills before he introduces a new unit or assignment so that the students build their comprehension skills while reading for information.
b. A science teacher recognizes that the students are having difficulty retaining information from their science textbooks when test time arrives. She creates a study guide with leading questions designed to help jog the students' memory about important concepts before the test.
c. Ms. Shannon, an art teacher, plans a field trip to see the latest exhibit featuring a symbolic artist. A language teacher at her school joins the students at the museum to lead a discussion about the function of symbols and their meanings, as well as different methods of interpreting shared symbols in a society.
d. A 1st-grade teacher uses children's books that introduce mathematical skills. For example, she reads a book weekly that tells a story about children preparing for a picnic, adding and subtracting items they need for the trip along the way. She encourages the children to solve the math questions along with her during the story.

15. Which of the following choices will be most important when designing a reading activity or lesson for students?

a. Selecting a text
b. Determining the number of students participating
c. Analyzing the point in the school year at which the lesson is given
d. Determining a purpose for instruction

16. A reading teacher is assessing an eighth grader to determine her reading level. Timed at a minute, the student reads with 93% accuracy. She misreads an average of seven words out of 100. What is her reading level?

a. She is reading at a Frustration level.
b. She is reading at a Listening level.
c. She is reading at an Instructional level.
d. She is reading at an Independent level.

17. Following instruction time, Ms. Pitman provides each student with a small sign that can be hung around the waist or neck. Ten children in her class receive signs displaying a single weekly vocabulary word. Five students get signs with the following: *dis-*, *re-*, *pre-*, *un-*, and *mis-*. The remaining students have signs with the following: *-ing*, *-ed*, *-s*, *-less*, and *-ful*. What is the best choice for a follow-up class activity based on this information?

a. The students are arranged into groups to demonstrate tangibly that certain parts of the English language have fixed functions.
b. Each student must use his or her sign to brainstorm a list of possible words that include those letters.
c. Each time a bell is rung, students must find a new partner with whom he or she can combine signs to make a new word.
d. Ask each student to explain what his or her sign means and how it functions in the English language.

Refer to the following for question 18:

Valeria is a bright sixth-grader who struggles with reading fluency. She comes from a predominantly Spanish-speaking home and has only lived in the United States for two years. Her teacher plans to use the guided oral reading strategy to help increase Valeria's reading skills. She also plans to use Valeria's scheduled media time to help work on her fluency.

18. Which of the following computer activities/games would be most beneficial to use during Valeria's media time?

a. Valeria can select from a variety of high-interest texts and read aloud what she sees on the screen.
b. Valeria can hear high-frequency sight and vocabulary words in her headphones and get points for "zapping" (clicking) the correct matching word on her screen.
c. Valeria can practice typing in a keyboarding program to build her speed and accuracy in writing reports and papers.
d. Valeria can surf a limited and pre-approved number of internet sites to read on subjects of her choosing.

19. Children develop phonological awareness:

a. Only through direct training given by adults
b. Only through natural exposure to language
c. Through both natural exposure and direct training
d. Through neither incidental exposure nor instruction

20. Silent reading fluency can best be assessed by:

a. Having the student retell or summarize the material to determine how much was understood.
b. Giving a written test that covers plot, theme, character development, sequence of events, rising action, climax, falling action, and outcome. A student must test at a 95% accuracy rate to be considered fluent at silent reading.
c. Giving a three-minute Test of Silent Contextual Reading Fluency four times a year. The student is presented with text in which spaces between words and all punctuation have been removed. The student must divide one word from another with slash marks, as in the example: The/little/sailboat/bobbed/so/far/in/the/distance/it/looked/like/a/toy. The more words a student accurately separates, the higher the silent reading fluency score.
d. Silent reading fluency cannot be assessed. It is a private act between the reader and the text and does not invite critique.

Refer to the following for question 21:

A class considers the paragraph below:

Sarah and Kelly grinned at one another conspiratorially as they approached Dad, who was quietly reading his paper in the living room. "Dad, we'd like to ride our bikes down to Emil's house today," giggled Kelly. She glanced at her sister and shifted her weight from foot to foot. Dad appeared to think this over for a moment and replied, "Sure, that's fine with me!" The girls scampered to get their bikes and were soon on their way. With the children gone, Dad noticed how peaceful and quiet the house sounded. His reverie was quickly interrupted as he heard Mom calling from upstairs, "okay, everybody, I told you at breakfast that I need as much help as I can get to help me give the dog a bath, clean the house and finish the laundry today!" Dad groaned, knowing that he had been conned!

21. Which method would be best for helping students determine the meaning of the word "reverie" in the next to last sentence?

a. Using context clues
b. Making an educated guess
c. Decoding the prefix, root, and suffix of the word
d. Previewing and reviewing

22. Of the following, which statement is true about instruction in the alphabetic principle?

a. Letter-sound relationships with the highest utility should be the earliest ones introduced.
b. The instruction of letter-sound correspondences should always be done in word context.
c. Letter-sound relationship practice times should only be assigned apart from other lessons.
d. Letter-sound relationship practice should focus on new relationships, not go over old ones.

23. The Alphabetic Principle is best defined as the concept that:

a. The letters of the alphabet are arranged in a specific sequence.
b. The letters of the alphabet are combined to spell various words.
c. The letters of the alphabet represent corresponding phonemes.
d. The letters of the alphabet are used to create matching sounds.

24. In a paired reading strategy for identifying the main idea in informational text, two students silently read a selection. Then, taking two-column notes of main ideas and supporting details, they take turns with the following steps. Which choice sequences these steps in the correct order?

a. The pair develops main idea consensus, a student paraphrases the main idea, a student explains agreement or disagreement, they take turns finding supporting details
b. A student paraphrases the main idea, a student explains agreement or disagreement, the pair develops main idea consensus, they take turns finding supporting details
c. They take turns finding supporting details, a student explains agreement or disagreement, a student paraphrases the main idea, the pair develops main idea consensus
d. A student explains agreement or disagreement, they take turns finding supporting details, the pair develops main idea consensus, a student paraphrases the main idea

25. Which of these correctly represents findings about research-based vocabulary instruction?

a. Children need word repetition consisting of drills for vocabulary development.
b. Children need only be exposed to new words once or twice to remember them.
c. Children learn the vocabulary in texts best indirectly through simply reading them.
d. Children require direct instruction and word exposure in various contexts.

26. A fourth-grade teacher had her students write haiku in order to promote the students' __________.

a. reading comprehension
b. vocabulary
c. word identification skills
d. confidence

27. Of the following, which represents an indirect way in which students receive instruction in and learn vocabulary?

a. Being exposed repeatedly to vocabulary in multiple teaching contexts
b. Being exposed to vocabulary when adults read aloud to them
c. Being pre-taught specific words found in text prior to reading
d. Being taught vocabulary words over extended periods of time

28. A syllable must contain:

a. A vowel
b. A consonant
c. Both a vowel and a consonant
d. A meaning

29. Which of the following is true about instructional approaches and activities for developing student phonological and phonemic awareness?

a. Direct, explicit instruction is the only effective method to teach manipulating phonemes in words.
b. Teachers cannot utilize informal interactions for these purposes because they are not systematic.
c. One instructional activity that is particularly suited for younger students is playing language games.
d. For younger students to identify spoken alliteration, they must first identify it in printed language.

30. To support student vocabulary development, which of the following most accurately describes the instructional materials teachers should use?

a. Teachers should only use literature and expository texts to support student vocabulary development.
b. Teachers should use newspapers, magazines, etc., in addition to literature and expository textbooks.
c. Teachers should use trade books, content-specific texts, and technology for vocabulary development.
d. Teachers should use a broad variety of instructional materials, including all of the above and others.

31. Which of the following is correct regarding phonological awareness in kindergarteners?

a. Children with delayed language development have benefited from phonological awareness training.
b. Researchers into instruction in phonological awareness advise against using SLPs and their methods.
c. Phonological awareness in kindergarteners requires changing phonemes in words to change meaning.
d. Phonological awareness instruction for kindergarteners involves only the individual phoneme level.

32. Which literary term describes the use of repeated vowel sounds in nearby words, such as in the sentence, "The splotchy drops dotted the window"?

a. Onomatopoeia
b. Alliteration
c. Consonance
d. Assonance

33. Some of the students in Mr. Smith's fourth-grade class cannot decode words well enough to read fluently in class. He knows they are well behind grade level and that he needs to provide them with activities that will allow them to be successful, building skills and confidence at the same time. Which activity would be best for this purpose?

a. Enlist the parents' help by sending home a weekly list of sight words that the students can practice and memorize, decreasing the need to decode when they read.
b. Show the students how to create words out of movable alphabet tiles or magnetic letters, building (encoding) words as they sound them out.
c. Provide the children with early childhood readers that contain only very simple words so that the children will not feel badly as they read.
d. Allow those children having trouble to stop each time they reach a challenging word and sound it out carefully, recording it to a list that will be studied for homework.

34. To help students decode words of increasing complexity, a teacher instructs them in strategies, including identifying Greek and Latin roots, prefixes, and suffixes to establish meaning. Which of the following does this strategy exemplify?

a. Alphabetic principle knowledge
b. Combinations of vowel sounds
c. Semantic and syntactic context
d. Structural cues in morphology

35. Maria's topic sentence is: "My family throws elaborate holiday celebrations." Which of the following would be the best supporting detail to follow that sentence?

a. Holidays are just a waste of everyone's time and money, in my opinion.
b. First, we decide who will host the holiday dinner and when the celebration will take place.
c. My household includes five people, but my extended family includes over thirty people.
d. Afterwards, we all help clean up and then relax by continuing to chat with each other.

36. One of the most important elements in children's literature that captures children's interest is

a. Character
b. Accuracy
c. Information
d. Vocabulary

37. Regarding story events in literary fiction, what is many authors' experience?

a. Story events help readers understand event causality instead of motives.
b. Story events are mental experiments that enable exploration for readers.
c. Story events most often define a specific meaning in life or a way of living.
d. Story events can explain motives and causes yet nothing of life's meaning.

38. In poetry, poems in which form are the shortest?

a. Ode
b. Epic
c. Elegy
d. Epigram

39. In Mr. Booker's first grade classroom, students are studying marine animals in science. Mr. Booker wants to select a book to read to the class that will enhance their understanding of this subject while at the same time capturing their interest in a story. Which of the following would be the best choice?

a. *The Wild Whale Watch*, part of the Magic School Bus series, a chapter book about whales
b. *The Whale Watchers Guide*, a book designed to help plan a whale-watching trip
c. *Moby Dick*, a famous 19th century novel about a man and a white whale
d. *The Pacific Ocean*, a book describing the ocean floor, tides, wave formation, and currents

40. Which of the following is true of literary character development?

a. Whether a character is dynamic or static is irrelevant to their development.
b. The main character's development throughout a story is usually the result of a conflict.
c. Round characters do not experience any development in a story.
d. Foils are used to make a main character's traits less obvious.

41. Which choice is the most correct statement about mood and tone in literature?

a. Mood and tone are synonyms referring to the emotional atmosphere of the work.
b. Mood is the emotion evoked in the reader by the work; tone is the author's emotion.
c. Mood is the emotion expressed by a work's author; tone is the emotion evoked in the reader by the work.
d. Mood is established by authors using different literary techniques than those used in creating tone.

42. Which of the following is true about the author's point of view in an informational text?

a. Readers can easily identify the author's point of view because informational texts include it as a main idea.
b. Readers often must infer the author's point of view because informational authors tend not to explicitly state it.
c. Readers may see the author's point of view equally well for neutral, balanced, and opinionated positions.
d. Readers who must analyze a text to identify the author's point of view can assume the text is poorly written.

43. In which stage of writing development do children understand that written forms symbolize meanings?

a. Scribbling and drawing
b. Letters
c. Letters and spaces
d. Letter-like forms and shapes

44. In writing instruction, what does the process writing approach entail?

a. Hypothetical audiences for written work
b. Students work on their own throughout.
c. Personal responsibility for written work
d. Writing is evaluated only by the teacher.

45. Based on research evidence, what do experts recommend to effectively instruct students in writing strategies?

a. Teachers should demonstrate strategies and then assign independent student practice.
b. Teachers should explain strategies and let students practice them without any models.
c. Teachers should model strategies, then guide practice, then give independent practice.
d. Teachers should first give students guided practice in strategies and then model them.

46. When using research-based writing instruction strategies, which should be gradually faded?

a. Brainstorming
b. Explicit instruction
c. Teacher modeling
d. Collaborative work

47. What does a writer do in the organization stage?

a. Determines the purpose, thesis, and supporting details of the written work
b. Brainstorms ideas for items to include in the written work
c. Submits the writing to a classmate for editing
d. Writes the introduction and conclusion

48. Which of the following should writers of fiction NOT do when writing dialogue?

a. Supply exposition in a subtle way
b. Imitate a real-life conversation verbatim
c. Use nonstandard spellings to show dialect
d. Provide more than a short break from narrative

49. Which of the following is NOT a method of peer editing?

a. Pairs of students analyze each others' sentences for variety.
b. Groups of students ask questions of the author to make the writing more clear.
c. Students work together to perform a final edit.
d. Students decide whether another student's essay is good writing or poor writing.

50. Which of these is most accurate about the function of dialogue in fictional literature?

a. Dialogue can serve to advance the plot but not develop characters.
b. Dialogue can serve to illuminate themes and meanings and redirect plots.
c. Dialogue can serve to break up exposition and slow the pace of the story.
d. Dialogue can serve to reproduce real speech instead of adding drama.

Social Science

51. Which of the following is NOT correct regarding assumptions of mercantilism?

a. The money and the wealth of a nation are identical properties.
b. In order to prosper, a nation should try to increase its imports.
c. In order to prosper, a nation should try to increase its exports.
d. Economic protectionism by national governments is advisable.

52. What does the data in this table most directly describe?

Inputs	1	2	3	4	5	6
Output	20	50	80	100	115	125

a. Law of diminishing marginal returns
b. Law of increasing opportunity cost
c. Law of demand
d. Law of marginal utility

53. Which of the following best defines American GDP?

a. The value, in American dollars, of all goods and services produced within American borders during one calendar year
b. The value, in American dollars, of all goods and services produced by American companies during one calendar year
c. The total value, in American dollars, of all American household incomes during one calendar year
d. The value, in American dollars, of a "market basket" of goods and services in one year divided by the value of the same market basket in a previous year multiplied by 100

54. Which social science focuses primarily on how a society produces and distributes goods?

a. Sociology
b. Anthropology
c. Psychology
d. Economics

55. In economic terms, which of the following is considered investment?

a. Buying a new home computer
b. Construction of a new manufacturing plant
c. Purchase of a college education
d. Selling finished goods to a customer

56. Which of the following exemplifies the multiplier effect of large cities?

a. The presence of specialized equipment for an industry attracts even more business.
b. The large population lowers the price of goods.
c. Public transportation means more people can commute to work.
d. A local newspaper can afford to give away the Sunday edition.

57. When the prices farmers receive for their crops decline in a developing country, this typically results in which of the following?

a. Increased urbanization
b. Increased college enrollment
c. Declining literacy rates
d. Higher prices for those crops in developed countries

58. A teacher tells the class that gasoline prices rose sharply in 2005 when Hurricane Katrina wiped out more than a quarter of crude oil production in the United States. The economic principle being taught in this lesson is the effect of:

a. Inflation
b. Deflation
c. Deficit spending
d. Supply and demand

59. Which of the following is an example of chemical weathering?

a. Frost wedging
b. Heat expansion
c. Acid rain
d. Salt wedging

60. How did Egypt's geographical features most contribute to the stability of ancient Egyptian civilization?

a. The Nile River regularly and predictably flooded, irrigating crops.
b. The expanse of the Nile River prevented Egyptians from settling elsewhere.
c. The Valley of the Kings divided Upper Egypt from Lower Egypt.
d. The Mediterranean Sea enabled contact between Egyptians and other ancient peoples.

61. The Erie Canal is 363 miles long and connects which body of water to Lake Erie?

a. The Mississippi River
b. The Hudson River
c. The Susquehanna River
d. The Lehigh River

62. Approximately what percentage of the Earth's surface is land?

a. 50
b. 10
c. 30
d. 85

63. Which of the following is true regarding the Tropic of Capricorn?

a. It separates the northern and southern hemispheres.
b. It separates the eastern and western hemispheres.
c. It is the southernmost latitude at which the sun can appear directly overhead at noon.
d. It is the northernmost latitude at which the sun can appear directly overhead at noon.

64. On which type of map are different countries represented in different colors, with no two adjacent countries sharing a color?

a. Physical map
b. Political map
c. Climate map
d. Contour map

65. All else being equal, which of the following locations is likely to have the coolest climate?

a. A city located at 6,000 feet above sea level
b. A city located at 500 feet above sea level
c. A city that receives less than 10 inches of precipitation per year
d. A city that receives more than 50 inches of precipitation per year

66. If you know the longitude of a city in the United States, what can you determine?

a. The state in which it is located
b. The time zone in which it is located
c. Exactly how far it is from the equator
d. Approximate average winter temperature

67. The Supreme Court has nine members. How is this number determined?

a. It is outlined in the Constitution.
b. Congress determines the number.
c. The President determines the number.
d. The Court decides on the number.

68. How must inferior courts interpret the law?

a. According to the Supreme Court's interpretation
b. According to the Constitution
c. However they choose
d. According to the political climate

69. How did the ruling in *Marbury v. Madison* alter the Supreme Court's power in the federal government?

a. It lessened it. The Supreme Court was concerned about the possibility of judges overturning laws enacted by voters through referendums and took away that power.
b. It increased it. The decision in *Marbury v. Madison* gave the Supreme Court its now traditional right to overturn legislation.
c. It increased it. The decision in *Marbury v. Madison* strengthened the Supreme Court's Constitutional right to overturn legislation.
d. There was no change. *Marbury v. Madison* was a case involving a president who was unwilling to obey laws enacted by his predecessor; there was nothing about the case or decision that would have more than a cursory connection to federal powers of government

70. How is a tie broken in the Senate?

a. The president pro tempore casts the deciding vote.
b. The Speaker of the House votes.
c. They vote again.
d. The vice president votes.

71. Most federal judges have served as local judges, lawyers, and law professors. These are ________ qualifications.

a. Formal
b. Required
c. Informal
d. Recommended

72. Power divided between local and central branches of government is a definition of what term?

a. Bicameralism
b. Checks and balances
c. Legislative oversight
d. Federalism

73. The Dred Scott case involved a Supreme Court ruling on:

a. Women's voting rights
b. Civil rights
c. Miranda Rights
d. Right to an attorney

74. The president serves as commander-in-chief. What are the president's two limitations in that role?

a. The president cannot declare war or make rules governing the military.
b. The president cannot enforce blockades or declare war.
c. The president cannot enforce quarantines or make rules governing the military.
d. The president cannot enforce blockades or quarantines.

75. How can Congress override the presidential veto of a bill?

a. By a majority vote in the House and a two-thirds majority in the Senate
b. By a two-thirds vote in the House and a majority in the Senate
c. By a majority vote in both the House and the Senate
d. By a two-thirds vote in both the House and the Senate

76. What grassroots political movement, started by southern and western farmers, arose in the 1890s US to fight banks, railroads, large corporations, and other "elites"?

a. Entrepreneurship Movement
b. Farmers United
c. Populist Movement
d. Social Gospel Movement

77. In the Progressive Era of the late 1890s and early 1900s, political reformers wanted to make sure government represented the people's will. An "initiative" process began in 1898 in South Dakota and then spread to other states. Which definition BEST describes the initiative process?

a. It allowed voting citizens to give their judgment on proposed legislation before state legislators voted on the same legislation.
b. It allowed voters to gather petitions demanding special elections when they wanted to recall an unpopular public official, thereby allowing them to "un-elect" that official.
c. It allowed citizens to introduce legislation proposals at a local or state level by gathering petitions, and proposals would then be addressed by lawmakers or placed on ballots for a vote.
d. It allowed citizens to visit state legislatures and give testimony supporting a certain issue, thereby encouraging the state lawmakers to propose and pass legislation on that same issue.

78. Which of the following is considered to be the largest cause of death among Native Americans following the arrival of European colonists in North America?

a. Wounds from wars with the European settlers
b. Wounds from wars with the other Native American tribes
c. European diseases
d. Exposure during the wintry, forced marches on which the European settlers forced them

79. Which of the following is true about Wilma Mankiller?

a. She was the first woman to win a Nobel prize and contributed to advancements in physics and chemistry.
b. She was a women's rights activist and improved Cherokee health care, education, and government as the principal chief of the Cherokee Nation.
c. She was an advocate for the education of women and children under Taliban occupation.
d. She was a civil rights activist known for her autobiographical works that detailed her experiences growing up as an African American woman.

80. How did Charlemagne's coronation as Holy Roman Emperor influence European politics?

a. It united much of Western Europe under a single ruler.
b. It strengthened papal authority regarding the right of political leaders to rule.
c. It made Catholicism the official religion throughout Charlemagne's empire.
d. It led to Charlemagne's renunciation of conquest by force.

81. Which of the following statements is NOT true of daily life for the average European in the 1500s?

a. Life was not significantly different from the medieval era.
b. The majority of people worked in agriculture.
c. Life expectancy was short.
d. Most people were literate, due to well-financed public education programs.

82. Which choice below lists some contributions to early America made by John Jay?

a. He was the first Chief Justice of New York and also a Minister to France.
b. He signed the Declaration of Independence and was one of the first mayors of New York City.
c. He served in George Washington's army during the Revolution and was Minister to Spain after the war.
d. He was a foreign minister, a contributing writer to the Federalist Papers, and an early governor of New York.

83. After the Civil War, urban populations increased. This growth was likely due to:

a. An increased reliance on agriculture
b. The Industrial Revolution
c. Prohibition
d. Slavery persisting in some areas

84. When President Warren Harding called for a "Return to Normalcy" in 1920, the best summary of what he meant would be:

a. A return to the high employment rate that had dominated the US during World War I
b. A return to peaceful times and a focus on domestic issues, as opposed to a focus on international war
c. A return to a period of high immigration rates that were contributing to a diverse culture and growing economy in the US
d. A return to finding more territories, like how Puerto Rico and Guam were acquired during the Spanish-American War, for expanding US markets

85. Which of the following statements is NOT true about the Gilded Age in America?

a. The Gilded Age was the era of the "robber barons" in the business world.
b. The Gilded Age got its name from the excesses of the wealthy upper class.
c. The Gilded Age had philanthropy Carnegie called the "Gospel of Wealth".
d. The Gilded Age is a term whose origins have not been identified clearly.

86. Which of the following ancient civilizations of the Americas lived in Central America?

a. The Incas
b. The Aztecs
c. The Mayans
d. All of these

87. Which of the following was the reason the economy of colonial New England focused mainly on manufacture and trade?

a. The soil and climate conditions in New England were not conducive to year-round farming.
b. The New England colonists were primarily merchants from England and Scotland.
c. Slavery did not exist in the northern colonies.
d. The New England colonists wanted to achieve economic dominance over the Middle Atlantic colonies.

88. Which skill should all students possess upon matriculating from elementary school into middle school?

a. The ability to identify different points of view related to a topic or event.
b. The ability to distinguish the difference between a primary and secondary source.
c. The ability to identify major eras in US history, beginning with colonization.
d. The ability to identify bias in written material.

Refer to the following for question 89:

> I was very young, but I remember sitting in our living room watching the television the day of the first moon landing, in 1969. It was a black and white television—my family didn't have a color one till later—and we all gathered in the room and watched the pictures. I'm not sure how they got the pictures to us, but I think it involved satellites around the earth they'd made especially for that purpose. The satellites captured the pictures and somehow beamed them into our televisions, live. That just showed again how our technology, American technology, had become much more advanced than Russian technology. The moon was pocked and pitted, like a big pumice stone. Watching Neil Armstrong walk on the moon was like nothing I'd ever imagined, and because of that somehow it was less surprising; I'd never thought it was impossible. Afterwards I went outside with my parents and my brother and we just kind of stared at the moon and imagined that people were on it, all those miles away.

89. For which of the following lesson units would this primary source be most appropriate?

a. Having students learn what it was like to witness the first moon landing
b. Teaching students about the surface of the moon
c. Teaching about the technology used to show the moon landing live on television
d. Having students learn about changes in television use

90. How could a teacher with 4th and 5th grade students put the concept of citizenship into a relevant context for her students?

a. Invite prominent citizens from the community to visit the class and speak about what citizenship means to the individual and the group.
b. Create a class "community" in which all students have jobs in the classroom and vote on issues important to the group.
c. Agree upon a class-wide service project through which students can help other in need.
d. Assign an essay topic requiring each student to write about "What Citizenship Means to Me."

91. To teach citizenship at the EC level, what purposes of laws and rules should teachers help young children to understand?

a. People who are employed in positions of authority wield unlimited powers.
b. Individual citizens determine their own responsibilities separately from laws.
c. Individuals and groups make up our government to create and enforce laws.
d. Life and society are unpredictable, insecure and disorderly, despite any laws.

92. Which of the following is accurate regarding chronological thinking in studying history?

a. Middle school students should be able to analyze patterns of historical succession.
b. Chronological thinking is necessary to see cause-and-effect relationships in history.
c. Students should not be expected to interpret data from timelines until high school.
d. Teachers should avoid using narratives to instruct younger students in chronology.

93. Of these materials, which can teachers use to help students develop chronological thinking?

a. Only history books can be used for this.
b. Biographies can also serve this function.
c. Historical literature can be used for this.
d. These are all good chronology materials.

Refer to the following for question 94:

A first-grade teacher is planning a geography unit focused on how the weather impacts the way that people live. This unit will focus on how weather differs in the regions near the poles, the tropical regions, and the mid-latitudes.

94. Which of the following introductory activities would be most aligned with an inquiry-based approach for instruction?

a. Reviewing the four seasons and having students draw and label each one
b. Incorporating seasonal clothing into the dramatic play area of the classroom
c. Asking students to name activities they can do in each type of weather
d. Displaying pictures of clothing from various climates around the world and leading a class discussion about their similarities and differences

95. Social studies education has many practical applications. Which of the following is the most direct application of teaching high school seniors the structure of the US government?

a. Knowledge of the fundamentals of federalism
b. Informed participation in school elections
c. Knowledge of a system of checks and balances
d. Informed participation in US political processes

Science

96. Which of these refers to the oceans and water areas of Earth?

a. Atmosphere
b. Hydrosphere
c. Exosphere
d. Lithosphere

97. Which type of rock typically forms on the surface of the Earth in cumulative layers?

a. Igneous
b. Obsidian
c. Metamorphic
d. Sedimentary

98. World weather patterns are most influenced by which of the following?

a. Wind belts

b. The Earth's orbit
c. Ocean currents
d. Atmospheric conditions

99. All of the following are true regarding wind energy, EXCEPT:

a. Wind turbines use space inefficiently, but they have low operational costs.
b. Wind is not a reliable source of energy in all geographic locations.
c. Wind turbines are expensive to manufacture and install.
d. Wind turbines are a threat to wildlife.

100. The majority of the solar energy that reaches Earth is absorbed by:

a. Glaciers
b. Landmasses
c. Oceans
d. The Earth's atmosphere

101. Which part of a hurricane features the strongest winds and greatest rainfall?

a. Eye wall
b. Front
c. Eye
d. Outward spiral

102. Which of the following is false regarding solar energy?

a. Solar energy is environmentally friendly
b. Solar energy has the greatest conversion efficiency
c. Solar energy is low maintenance
d. Solar energy is silent

103. Which of the following statements is NOT congruent with the theory of plate tectonics?

a. The continents were once connected in the large supercontinent Pangea.
b. The tectonic plates are part of the Earth's lithosphere.
c. Seafloor spreading is evidence of tectonic plate movement.
d. Subduction occurs at divergent boundaries.

104. The distance from the earth to the sun is equal to which of the following?

a. One astronomical unit
b. One light-year
c. One parsec
d. One arcsecond

105. How are lipids different from other organic molecules?

a. They consist of repeating monomers to form long chains.
b. They are not water soluble.
c. They serve as catalysts.
d. Lipids store less energy per gram than carbohydrates or proteins.

106. Plants begin to break down the products of photosynthesis through respiration. What is the result of respiration?

a. Water
b. Oxygen and glucose
c. Carbon dioxide and sugar
d. Carbon dioxide and water

107. Which of the following would not be used as evidence for evolution?

a. Fossil record
b. DNA sequences
c. Anatomical structures
d. Reproductive habits

108. What type of mutation is represented by the following sequence?

Original: 1 2 3 4 5 6
Mutated: 1 5 4 3 2 6

a. Breakage
b. Deletion
c. Insertion
d. Inversion

109. This organelle contains digestive enzymes that break down food and unneeded substances. They are also thought to be linked to the aging process. What part of a cell does this describe?

a. Lysosomes
b. Chromatin
c. Plastids
d. Golgi apparatus

110. Which of the following body systems allows a person to move?

a. integumentary system
b. digestive system
c. endocrine system
d. muscular system

111. When an animal takes in more energy than it uses over an extended time, the extra chemical energy is stored as:

a. Fat
b. Starch
c. Protein
d. Enzymes

112. Which of the following molecules is thought to have acted as the first enzyme in early life on earth?

a. Protein
b. RNA
c. DNA
d. Triglycerides

113. Which of the following best describes the primary function of carbohydrates?

a. Provide energy
b. Aid in metabolism
c. Muscle tissue function
d. Prevents cell damage

114. Prokaryotic and eukaryotic cells are similar in having which of the following?

a. Membrane-bound organelles
b. Protein-studded DNA
c. Presence of a nucleus
d. Integral membrane proteins in the plasma membrane

115. Which of the following substances has a pH closest to 1?

a. Bleach
b. Water
c. Ammonia
d. Vinegar

116. Which of the following statements about heat transfer is NOT true?

a. As the energy of a system changes, its thermal energy must change or work must be done.
b. Heat transfer from a warmer object to a cooler object can occur spontaneously.
c. Heat transfer can never occur from a cooler object to a warmer object.
d. If two objects reach the same temperature, energy is no longer available for work.

117. How do the hydrogen bonds in water affect its characteristics?

a. Hydrogen bonds are so polar that they can attract non-polar molecules.
b. Hydrogen bonds cause water to be denser when it is a solid than when it is a liquid.
c. Hydrogen bonds cause water to have a high enough surface tension that some organisms can move across it.
d. Hydrogen bonds cause water to be a poor solvent.
e. Hydrogen bonds make water an excellent buffer.

118. Which of the following subatomic particles has the smallest mass?

a. Protons
b. Electrons
c. Quarks
d. Neutrons

119. Which of the following is the best prediction for solubility at 150 degrees Celsius?

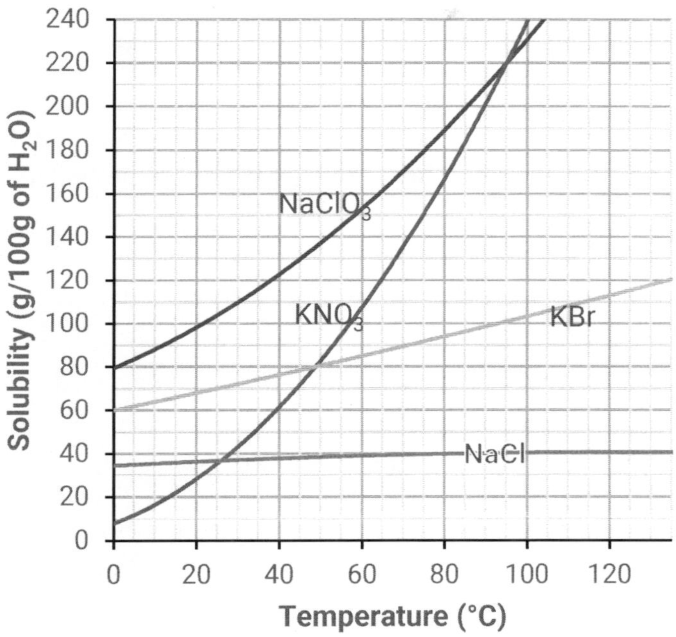

a. 260 g $NaClO_3$ per 100 g H_2O
b. 250 g KNO_3 per 100 g H_2O
c. 130 g KBr per 100 g H_2O
d. 80 g NaCl per 100 g H_2O

120. A piece of art with a mass of 200 kg is suspended from two nails so that the angle the hanging wires make is 40° with the horizontal. What is the tension in the hanging wires? (Note: $\sin 40° = 0.6428$ and $\cos 40° = 0.7660$).

a. 1,279 N
b. 1,525 N
c. 1,960 N
d. 3,049 N

121. Students experimentally determine that the specific heat of copper is $0.410 \frac{J}{g \cdot °C}$. If the known value of the specific heat of copper is $0.385 \frac{J}{g \cdot °C}$, what is the percent error?

a. 6.10%
b. 16.4%
c. 6.49%
d. 15.4%

122. Which of the following statements is NOT true about the period of a simple pendulum?

a. As the mass of a pendulum increases, the period increases.
b. For small amplitudes, the period of a pendulum is approximately independent of amplitude.
c. A pendulum swings more slowly at higher elevation.
d. To double the period of a pendulum, the length must be quadrupled.

123. Which of the following is a solute?

a. Salt in a mixture of salt and pepper
b. Air in a mixture of ash and air
c. Water in a mixture of salt and water
d. Sugar in a mixture of sugar and water

124. Which of the following wastes may be suitable for sink or sewer disposal?

a. Acetic acid
b. Benzene
c. Acetone
d. Mercury

125. Basic principles for EC teachers to help children learn via scientific inquiry and discovery include:

a. Using learning materials created by experts, not from everyday environments
b. Concentrating on getting children to observe more than observing themselves
c. Using materials in structured activities before they let children play with them
d. Teaching what they know by using materials with which they are most familiar

126. Which is the best definition of an informal learning experience for learning basic science concepts?

a. A child chooses what to do, and an adult provides some intervention
b. A child chooses what to do spontaneously without adult intervention
c. A child engages in an activity which is chosen and directed by an adult
d. A child engages in a group activity assigned by the preschool teacher

127. When working in the laboratory, what is the minimum length of time an eye should be flushed if a chemical gets in the eye?

a. 2 minutes
b. 10 minutes
c. 15 minutes
d. 30 minutes

128. Which of these is NOT a general process skill that EC science programs should help develop?

a. Dissection
b. Observation
c. Classification
d. Communication

Refer to the following for question 129:

A sixth-grade science teacher tells her students that they will have a seismologist studying plate tectonics come to class. She has a group of early-intermediate English learners in her class. The seismologist will discuss what causes earthquakes, the effects of earthquakes, and any questions students might have on the topic.

129. One student wants to know what causes the shaking that occurs with an earthquake. What answer would the seismologist likely give to that student?

a. Static deformation
b. Seismic waves
c. Compression waves
d. Continental drift

130. When students are taught science, the information needs to be:

a. Correct, contextualized, and explained
b. Diverse, multicultural, and functional
c. Demonstrated, teacher-prepared, and manipulative
d. Theoretical, practical, and researched

131. A kindergarten teacher places several toy animal figurines into the science area of the classroom and asks students to identify distinguishing features as they play, such as a duck's webbed feet, an elephant's trunk, or a bird's feathers. This strategy is most likely intended to use models for developing students' initial understanding of which of the following scientific concepts?

a. Heredity
b. Constancy and change
c. Adaptation
d. Land and aquatic habitats

132. To introduce a unit on the impact of litter on the environment, a kindergarten teacher leads the class in picking up trash from the school playground. Which of the following additional activities would be most effective in demonstrating this concept for students of this age group?

a. Placing the trash items into a bin of water for students to observe the effects
b. Having students sort recyclable versus nonrecyclable materials
c. Repurposing the trash items for an art activity
d. Discussing the difference between toxic and nontoxic materials

133. Which of the following is a characteristic of a reputable scientific journal?

a. Peer review of the quality of research
b. Famous scientists on the editorial board
c. Use of color graphics to represent data
d. Statistical analysis of all research data

134. Once a hypothesis has been verified and accepted, it becomes which of the following?

a. A fact
b. A law
c. A conclusion
d. A theory

135. Which of the following subskills best fits the process skill of observing?

a. Using the five senses to collect evidence and write descriptions
b. Grouping objects based on similarities, differences, and interrelationships

c. Explaining or interpreting collected evidence
d. Reporting to others what has been found by experimentation

136. Which of the following is needed for an experiment to be considered successful?

a. A reasonable hypothesis
b. A well-written lab report
c. Data that others can reproduce
d. Computer-aided statistical analysis

137. Which set of scientific thinkers is related to the study of chemistry?

a. Newton, Einstein, Feynman, and Hawking
b. Hooke, Pasteur, Watson & Crick, and Jacob & Monod
c. Ibn Hayyan, Lavoisier, Mendeleev, and Curie
d. Hutton, Darwin, Cuvier, and Wegener

138. Mrs. Jones's class conducted an experiment on the effects of sugar and artificial sweetener on the cookie recipe's overall color when baked. What would be the independent variable in the cookie experiment?

a. The students should use the same ingredients in both recipes, but bake the cookies with sugar at 450 degrees and those with artificial sweetener at 475 degrees. They should increase the baking time on the artificial sweetener cookies, since the package instructs them to do so
b. The students should use the same ingredients in both recipes, but increase the baking time on the artificial sweetener cookies, since the package instructs them to do so
c. The students should use the same ingredients, same baking temperatures, and same baking times for both recipes
d. The students should use the same ingredients and baking times in both recipes, but bake the cookies with sugar at 450 degrees and the artificial sweetener cookies at 475 degrees

139. In the scientific method, which of the following steps should come first?

a. Formulating a hypothesis
b. Asking a research question
c. Conducting an experiment
d. Reporting support or refutation

140. Which of the following is NOT a characteristic of scientific inquiry?

a. Continual posing of questions and testing of hypotheses
b. Objective analysis of experimental data
c. Ongoing peer review of shared information
d. The assumption that published literature is accurate and unbiased

Mathematics

141. What linear equation includes the data in the table below?

x	y
−3	1
1	−11
3	−17
5	−23
9	−35

a. $y = -3x - 11$
b. $y = -6x - 8$
c. $y = -3x - 8$
d. $y = -12x - 11$

142. Quinn deposits $250 from each quarterly paycheck into a savings account. How much will he have deposited in the account after 5 years?

a. $4,800
b. $5,000
c. $5,200
d. $5,400

143. Which of the following graphs represents the solution to the system of inequalities below?

$$-2x + 3y \leq 3$$
$$-8x + 6y \geq -3$$

a.

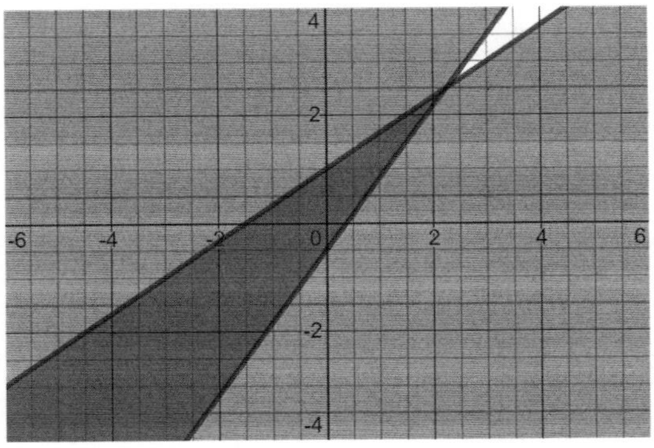

b.

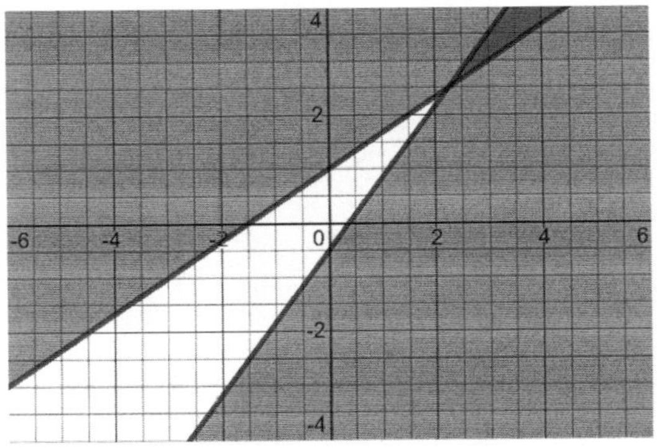

c.

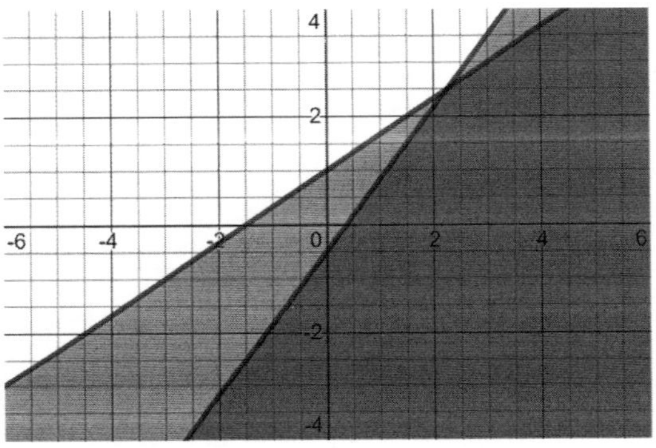

d.

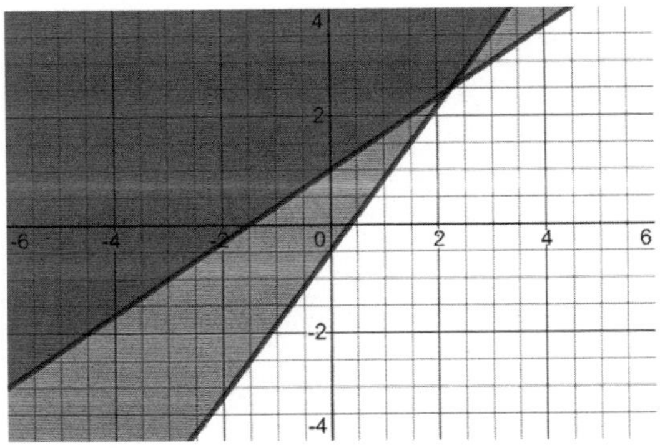

144. Solve $\sqrt{2x} - 3 = \sqrt{2x - 15}$.

a. $x = 0$
b. $x = 4$
c. $x = 8$
d. $x = 10$

145. Hannah spends at least \$16 on 4 packages of coffee. Which of the following expresses this relationship in terms of the cost of a package of coffee, p?

a. $16 \geq 4p$
b. $16 < 4p$
c. $16 > 4p$
d. $16 \leq 4p$

146. How many square feet of paint would be needed to cover a globe with a radius of 7.5 inches?

a. 1.04
b. 4.91
c. 128.6
d. 706.5

147. Which of these is NOT a net of a cube?

a. b. c. d.

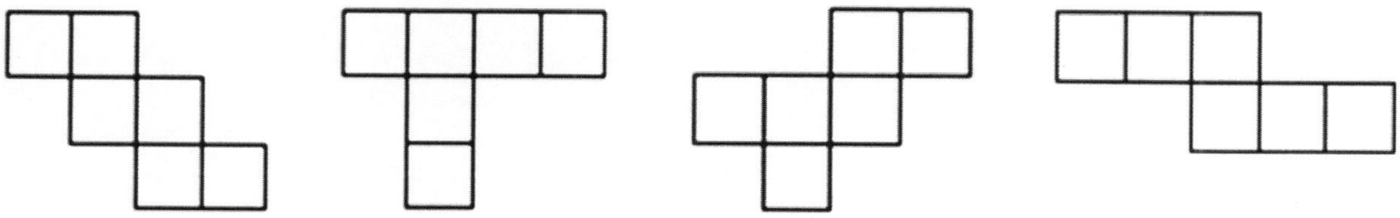

148. The total perimeter of an L-shaped field is 800 feet. The longest side is 300 feet, and the longest width is 100 feet. Each of the shorter sides is 50 feet. What is the total area of the field?

a. 17,500 square feet
b. 22,500 square feet
c. 30,000 square feet
d. 45,000 square feet

149. A 24-foot-tall building casts a shadow that is 6 feet in length. If a dog next to the building casts a shadow 0.75 feet long, how tall is the dog?

a. 1.5 feet
b. 2 feet
c. 2.5 feet
d. 3 feet

150. What is the area of the parallelogram in the figure below?

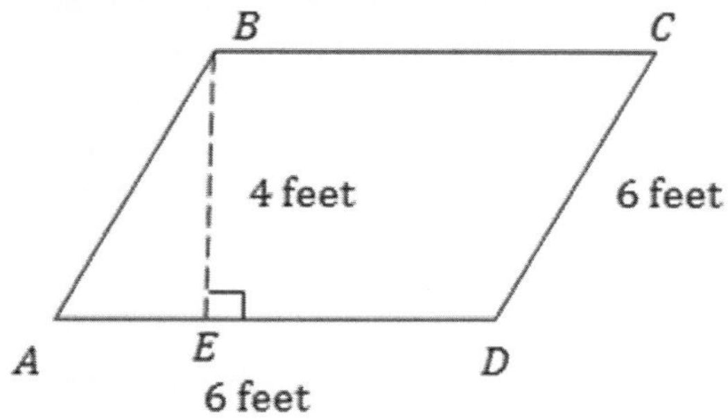

a. 12 square feet
b. 24 square feet
c. 36 square feet
d. 144 square feet

151. Kyra sets aside $\frac{1}{3}$ of her income to pay rent and utilities at her apartment. If the monthly cost of rent and utilities is $1,050, what is her monthly salary?

a. $3,150
b. $3,225
c. $3,750
d. $4,050

152. Herbert plans to use the earnings from his lemonade stand, according to the table below, for the first month of operations. If he buys $70 worth of lemons, how much profit does he take home?

Cash Flow Item	Percentage of Total Earning Used on Item
Lemons	35%
Sugar	20%
Cups	25%
Stand improvements	5%
Profits	15%

a. $15
b. $20
c. $30
d. $35

153. Sophia is at the market buying fruit for her family of four. Kiwifruit is only sold in packages of three. If Sophia would like each family member to have the same number of kiwifruits, which of the following approaches can Sophia use to determine the fewest number of kiwifruits she should buy?

a. Sophia needs to determine the greatest common multiple of 3 and 4.
b. Sophia needs to determine the least common multiple of 3 and 4.
c. Sophia needs to determine the least common divisor of 3 and 4.
d. Sophia needs to determine the greatest common divisor of 3 and 4.

154. A student is presented with the following problem: $4^2 + 5(4 \times 3) - 10$. Which operation should the student perform first?

a. Multiplying five by four and three
b. Squaring four
c. Subtracting ten from three
d. Adding four and five

155. Which of the following correctly compares the sets of whole numbers and counting numbers?

a. The sets of whole and counting numbers are equal.
b. The sets of whole and counting numbers are disjoint.
c. The set of whole numbers is a subset of the set of counting numbers.
d. The set of counting numbers is a subset of the set of whole numbers.

156. Ms. Chen is instructing her students on divisibility rules. Which of the following rules can be used to determine if a number is divisible by 6?

a. The last digit of the number is divisible by 2 or 3.
b. The number ends in 6.
c. The number is divisible by 2 and 3.
d. The last two digits of the number are divisible by 6.

157. In the mathematical order of operations, which of these is true?

a. Exponents are done before adding, subtracting, multiplying, or dividing.
b. Calculations outside of parentheses are done before those inside of them.
c. Addition and subtraction are done before multiplication and division.
d. Multiplication is done before division, and addition is before subtraction.

158. Mrs. Vories, a fifth-grade teacher, asks her class to use compatible numbers to help her determine approximately how many chicken nuggets she needs to buy for a school-wide party. The school has 589 students and each student will be served nine nuggets. Which student correctly applied the concept of compatible numbers?

a. Madison estimates: $500 \times 10 = 5{,}000$ nuggets
b. Audrey estimates: $600 \times 5 = 3{,}000$ nuggets
c. Ian estimates: $600 \times 10 = 6{,}000$ nuggets
d. Andrew estimates: $500 \times 5 = 2{,}500$ nuggets

159. Olivia receives her weekly paycheck and calculates that she will spend $\frac{1}{4}$ of it on groceries. If the groceries cost $120, what is the amount of her paycheck?

a. $360
b. $425
c. $480
d. $600

160. Which of the following correctly compares the sets of rational numbers and integers?

a. The sets of rational numbers and integers are equal.
b. The sets of rational numbers and integers are disjoint.
c. The set of integers is a subset of the set of rational numbers.
d. The set of rational numbers is a subset of the set of integers.

161. Suppose Olivia rolls a regular six-sided die 10 times. How many times can she expect to roll a 4?

a. $\frac{3}{4}$
b. $\frac{5}{2}$
c. $\frac{5}{3}$
d. $\frac{8}{9}$

162. A student scores 68 on a final exam. Another student scores 84 on the exam. The class average is 80, with a standard deviation of 8 points. Assuming the distribution is normal, what percentage of the class scored within the range of these two students' scores?

a. 44.32%
b. 48.54%
c. 58.39%
d. 62.47%

163. Seven samples were obtained having the values 21, 22, 26, 29, 27, 26 and 24. The mean and standard deviation values are:

a. 22.4 and 2.8
b. 25 and 2.2
c. 25 and 2.8
d. 25.6 and 2.2

164. Abram rolls a 6-sided die with each side labeled 1–6. What is the probability he rolls an even number or a number greater than 4?

a. $\frac{1}{6}$
b. $\frac{2}{3}$
c. $\frac{3}{4}$
d. $\frac{5}{6}$

165. What is the average of 2.02, 0.275, and 1.98?

a. 1.1375
b. 1.375
c. 1.425
d. 2.25

166. Of the following, which is a prerequisite for young children to understand before they can engage in accurately estimating basic measurements of quantities?

a. Knowledge of math vocabulary words indicating estimation
b. Knowledge of how to make predictions that are appropriate
c. Knowledge of how to achieve estimates that are reasonable
d. Knowledge of what relative quantities and comparisons are

167. Which of the following is NOT a model that helps students understand subtraction?

a. Take away
b. Missing addend
c. Number line
d. Adding zero

168. Of the following, what statement is correct regarding practice in measurement for young children?

a. Measurement is exclusively a formal method for quantifying sizes, time durations, weights, etc.
b. Measurement is for both formal quantification and recognizing and finding real-life relationships.
c. Measurement can only be accomplished by young children with standard measurement devices.
d. Measurement practice for young children is unlikely to help them in learning about comparisons.

169. Of the following, which is/are NOT an example(s) of math manipulatives?

a. Tangrams for shape recognition
b. Large magnetic number boards
c. Printed mathematical formulas
d. Play money and toy cash registers

170. A missing object problem like the one below is one way of helping students learn what concept?

Truck car bike train truck car bike ______ truck car bike train

a. Counting
b. Problem solving
c. Manipulation of objects
d. Basic addition

171. Which of the following would be most effective to help young children learn geometry?

a. Giving them hands-on activities manipulating concrete objects
b. Giving them the earliest geometric theorems to memorize
c. Giving them everyday life activities only after they learn basics
d. Giving them instructions for drawing geometric shape diagrams

172. Which of the following learning goals is most appropriate for a fourth-grade unit on geometry and measurement?

a. The students will be able to use a protractor to determine the approximate measures of angles in degrees to the nearest whole number.
b. The students will be able to describe the process for graphing ordered pairs of numbers in the first quadrant of the coordinate plane.
c. The students will be able to determine the volume of a rectangular prism with whole number side lengths in problems related to the number of layers times the number of unit cubes in the area of the base.
d. The students will be able to classify two-dimensional figures in a hierarchy of sets and subsets using graphic organizers based on their attributes and properties.

173. When children develop good problem-solving skills, how does this affect related characteristics?

a. Problem-solving skills promote abilities with self-regulation.
b. Problem-solving skills promote rigidity more than flexibility.
c. Problem-solving skills promote quick action over periods of deliberation.
d. Problem-solving skills promote an increase in more dangerous risk taking.

174. A teacher is assessing the students' understanding of the appropriate units for length, area, and volume. Which of the following only lists units of area?

a. in^2, mm^2, ft^2
b. yd, yd^2, yd^3
c. mm, cm, m
d. m^2, s^2, km^2

175. A third-grade student's continuous inability to do which of the following may indicate the potential need for further evaluation?

a. Multiply three-digit whole numbers
b. Compare and order fractions
c. Divide two-digit whole numbers
d. Add and subtract whole numbers within 100

Answer Key and Explanations for Test #2

Language Arts and Reading

1. B: Typical speech is roughly 125 words per minute, while typical thinking is estimated at roughly 500 words per minute. This natural disparity does not make listening less effective than reading. While the slower rate of speech and the faster rate of thought does allow students' minds to wander, teachers can have students make use of this time by instructing them to summarize mentally the speech they hear as an active listening technique. This enables students to process, consider, and manipulate heard information and make richer, more creative decisions about it. Listening and learning share the common characteristics of being both social and reciprocal.

2. A: In (A), the teacher guides previewing of information to show students how to put themselves in the right frame of mind to listen carefully for meaning. Students are then able to listen in a guided way based upon the previewing. By varying the type of comprehension assessment, the teacher will get a better understanding of what the students learned. (B) is a good exercise but does not provide for direct instruction by the teacher or a particularly skilled student. In (C), students are focusing more on reading comprehension than listening since they must read the story to themselves and then write a report. There is then no way to gauge what they have learned. (D) would be useful but does not include teacher-guided previewing, which is very helpful in building comprehension.

3. C: For internet sources, the name of the author can usually be found, but it may not be obvious at first. Therefore, choice C is correct; those wishing to cite the author may need to Internet search more thoroughly than usual to find the author's name. Nevertheless, they should not immediately assume the author is not named, so choice A is incorrect. Many internet sources are published by government agencies or private corporations and do not provide individual author names. In these cases, the writer should not list an author at all, so choice B is incorrect. Online sources omit authors' names much more commonly than do print sources. In these cases, citing the title in lieu of the author's name is not just allowed but advised by the MLA, so choice D is incorrect.

4. A: The best source for information would be a medical journal. While the other sources may have information on the topic, the medical journal would have the most reliable information.

5. B: Choice B is correct, as natural communication is generally ideal in public speaking, and verbal and nonverbal communication alike should be natural. Choice A is incorrect because speakers should practice their speeches extensively to ensure confidence and ease of delivery; they will not be received as spontaneous in a good way if they stumble, search for words, or stop to consult notes. Choice C is incorrect because the use of humor can be used to engage with the audience and keep their attention. Although too much humor could be distracting, it is a good tool for audience engagement when used appropriately. Choice D is incorrect because random or irrelevant movements (such as hair-twirling, foot-tapping, pencil-tapping, face-rubbing, etc.) will distract the audience rather than engage them.

6. D: Mobile and text media are very popular (a) and increasingly so, an advantage for effective public communications. Another advantage of text messaging using mobile phones is the timeliness (b) with which information and reminders can be sent. Especially for public communications intended to effect social change, their interactive (c) potential is an additional advantage. Other advantages include decreasing costs and increasing rural reach. One disadvantage of this media format is the limited length (d) to which messages are restricted. However, most presenters work around this disadvantage by inserting hyperlinks to websites/webpages for accessing further information. Other disadvantages include provider charges, although today, more providers are including free texting in mobile plans.

7. C: The bandwagon method appeals to audiences to use a brand because it is popular, implying popularity indicates quality. Past Dr Pepper® commercials sang, "I'm a pepper, he's a pepper, she's a pepper.... Wouldn't you like to be a pepper, too?" Associating a car with a beautiful model (a), a soap with a waterfall (b), or a USA-made brand with an American flag (d) are all examples of the transfer method of appeal: viewers transfer the feelings they get from symbols to associated products and (unconsciously/consciously) want the products to get those feelings.

8. B: A maze test is a specific type of cloze test. In a cloze test, words are deleted, and the reader must supply the missing words using contextual clues and vocabulary that is familiar. A maze test is essentially a multiple-choice application of a cloze test.

9. B: The 3N strategy does use scaffolding, i.e., temporary support that the teacher provides to help young students achieve tasks at levels higher than their current literacy status. Scaffolding is gradually withdrawn as students become more proficient until they can achieve these tasks independently. 3N *does* incorporate informal assessment of literacy levels (A): the first, "Notice" step involves the teacher's noticing each individual student's current level of literacy skills. It *does* integrate reflection (C): the third, "Narrate" step involves the teacher's reflecting on what the student does. This strategy *is* adaptable to young children's games (D): various literacy games designed for young children apply the 3N strategy.

10. C: This method is likely to fail, producing students at a Frustration reading level. Those reading below grade level are likely to give up entirely. Those reading at grade level are likely to get frustrated and form habits that will actually slow down their development. Giving students texts that are too far beyond their reach produces frustrated readers. In an effort to succeed, frustrated readers are likely to apply strategies that have worked for them in the past but cannot work in this case because the text is simply beyond them. Looking for contextual clues to understand the meaning of unfamiliar words requires that most of the words in the passage are familiar. Breaking unfamiliar words into individual phonemes or syllables can be effective, but not if the number of such words is excessive. In this case, students below reading level and students at reading level will become frustrated when the skills that have worked for them in the past now fail.

11. D: Research finds that most teachers can plan differentiated instruction based on the findings of studies, and that they do this better when using individual scores of real students than with invented scores of hypothetical students. Research has found that teachers make data-based instructional decisions better in small groups than individually, not vice versa. Studies show that most teachers can locate data in graphs or tables, but have more trouble with data comprehension than vice versa. Research also finds that the majority of teachers have difficulty with both interpreting relationships among variables and posing questions.

12. C: One of the advantages of portfolio assessments is that they can be used both as formative assessments and as summative assessments, so choice C is correct. A teacher can review a student's latest writing sample in a portfolio to gauge current performance levels, compare it to the sample immediately before it, and thereby make a formative assessment. On the other hand, a teacher can review all contents of a portfolio collected over an entire school year to assess overall achievement as a summative assessment. Since portfolio assessments are not limited to being formative or summative, choices A and B are incorrect, and since portfolio assessments can be formative or summative, choice D is incorrect.

13. C: To get data to inform a school improvement plan (a), a teacher could use a summative assessment, comparing student scores at the end of the school year to their baseline scores obtained at the beginning of that year. This can also be done to show accountability to the federal government (e.g., meeting adequate yearly progress criteria) to get or keep school funding (b); and to get data on student progress toward instructional objectives over the entire school year (d). A teacher would use a formative assessment to get data about individual student performance (c); summative assessments yield more group data and less individual data.

14. B: Integrated curriculum is vital to student growth and to fostering a love of learning. In reality, all subject areas are related, and a good teacher will find ways to highlight the connection of concepts across the curriculum. In choice B, the science teacher provides a way to help students study for a test. However, she would probably be better advised to work with the students on comprehension and retention before test time arrives. She could use a variety of previewing and reviewing skills, as well as creative ways to bring the information to life during class discussions and activities. This teacher might also benefit from discussing the situation with a language arts teacher to get ideas on how to build skills in reading for information, main ideas, and supporting concepts.

15. D: It is impossible to include every text desired into the language curriculum—there are simply too many good books, stories, poems, speeches, and media available. Teachers must first think about what skills their students need to acquire, as well as what skills they have already mastered. In designing activities for class, a good teacher will start first with the purpose for instruction. For example, purposes of reading can include: reading for information, reading for enjoyment, understanding a message, identifying main or supporting ideas, or developing an appreciation for artistic expression/perception. Once the purpose or intended learning outcome has been identified, the teacher will have a much better idea of which texts, strategies, and activities will support that purpose.

16. C: In one minute, a student who misreads one or less than one word per twenty words, or with 95%–100% accuracy, is at an Independent reading level. A student who misreads one or less than one word per ten words, or with 90%–95% accuracy, is at an Instructional level. A student misreading more than one word out of ten, or with less than 90% accuracy, is at a Frustration level.

17. C: One-half of the class receives signs showing vocabulary words, which are probably used as root words. The remaining students are split into two general groups: those with prefixes on their signs and those with suffixes. The best approach is to get the students moving, listening, and talking in order to solidify their understanding of how roots, suffixes, and prefixes work together to make new meanings out of various root words. This approach also allows the students to participate in a game in a group context, making the activity more fun and engaging.

18. B: Reading fluency refers to the speed, inflection and accuracy with which students read, either orally or silently. In order to read fluently, students must be able to decode, or break down into segments, words that adhere to the common rules of the English alphabet. For those words that are generally not easily decoded, students must build their vocabulary of "sight words," which should be recognized without the need to decode. In (A), students may or may not be reading fluently or accurately, since the computer program does not monitor how the student reads. In (C), keyboarding practice bears no direct relationship to reading fluency. In (D), again, the computer is simply a source for text, but does not build any specific fluency skill. In (B), students are exposed to sight words and vocabulary in a fun way. Using a computer program allows for an unlimited supply of relevant words and for accurate scoring.

19. C: Children develop phonological awareness through a combination of incidental learning from natural exposure to language in their environments and from direct instruction from adults. They do not develop it solely through one or the other, nor do they develop it without either of these methods.

20. C: Silent reading fluency can be monitored over time by giving the Test of Silent Contextual Reading Fluency (TSCRF) four times a year. A similar assessment tool is the Test of Silent Word Reading Fluency (TOSWRF), in which words of increasing complexity are given as a single, undifferentiated, and unpunctuated strand. As with the TSCRF, three minutes are given for the student to separate each word from the next. *Itwillcannotschoolbecomeagendaconsistentphilosophysuperfluous* is an example of such a strand.

21. A: The text at hand contains several clues as to the meaning of this word, including the use of the words "peaceful" and "quiet" in the preceding sentence. Students may also recognize that Mom's requests for help with undesirable household chores interrupted Dad's peaceful, quiet 'reverie." Choice A is the specific method that would be most appropriate for determining the word's meaning; Choice B is a less reliable or systematic way of doing the same thing. Choice C would not be helpful in this case since "reverie" is not a word that can be decoded in a traditional manner. Choice D would not offer a realistic solution to this question since previewing and reviewing are more helpful in increasing comprehension of informative texts, rather than vocabulary words.

22. A: While there is no consensus among experts as to any universal sequence of instruction for teaching the alphabetic principle through phonics instruction, they do agree that, to enable children to start reading words as soon as possible, the highest-utility relationships should be introduced earliest. For example, the letters *m, a, p, t,* and *s* are all used frequently, whereas the *x* in *box*, the sound of *ey* in *they*, and the letter *a* when pronounced as it is in *want* have lower-utility letter-sound correspondences. Important considerations for the alphabetic principle are to teach letter-sound correspondences in isolation, not in word contexts; to teach them explicitly; to give students opportunities to practice letter-sound relationships within their other daily lessons, not only separately; and to include cumulative reviews of relationships taught earlier along with new ones in practice opportunities.

23. C: The best definition of the Alphabetic Principle is that the letters of the alphabet are symbols to represent the various phonemes (speech sounds) we use in our language. While it is true that the alphabet has a sequence (A), this does not define the Alphabetic Principle. The sequence serves as a master mnemonic to help us remember all the letters, but we could still identify letters and associate them with phonemes without it. Similarly, choice B is true but is not the definition. Choice D is the reverse of the correct answer (sounds => letters, not letters => sounds).

24. B: In this paired reading strategy, which improves reading comprehension and helps students identify the main idea in informational text, after silently reading a text selection, the pair of students takes turns following these steps: One student paraphrases what he or she thinks the text's main idea is. The other student agrees or disagrees, explaining why. The pair then develops a consensus as to the text's main idea. Then they take turns finding details in the text that support its main idea.

25. D: Research-based vocabulary instruction findings show that children need ample word repetition, but not through drilling. Multiple exposures to the same words in different contexts are more effective. Multiple and repeated exposures are important because children do not learn vocabulary through only one or two exposures to a new word. Research finds that they do not simply learn vocabulary in texts indirectly from reading; instead, teachers must give them direct instruction in the new vocabulary words they find in their texts.

26. B: Writing haikus will promote students' vocabularies. The tightly controlled syllabic requirements will cause students to search for words outside their normal vocabularies that will fit the rigid framework and still express the writer's intended meanings. Often, students will rediscover a word whose meaning they know, but they don't often use.

27. B: Indirect ways in which students receive instruction and learn vocabulary include through daily conversations, reading on their own, and being read aloud to by adults. Direct instruction and learning in vocabulary include teachers providing extended instruction exposing students repeatedly to vocabulary words in multiple teaching contexts, teachers pre-teaching specific words found in text prior to students reading it, and teachers instructing students over extended time periods and having them actively work with vocabulary words.

28. A: A syllable is a minimal sound unit arranged around a vowel. For example, *academic* has four syllables: *a/ca/dem/ic.* It is possible for a syllable to be a single vowel, as in the above example. It is not possible for a syllable to be a single consonant.

29. C: Playing language games helps younger students to develop phonological and phonemic awareness while having fun, which better motivates them to learn. For example, teachers can ask children to see how many different rhyming words they can produce by changing the initial sound of a given word (e.g., cat, hat, mat, fat, sat, pat, bat, rat, vat, etc.). Hence manipulating phonemes in words not only can be taught in different ways, it *should* be taught using a variety of approaches and materials. Such approaches include utilizing informal interactions: these provide a meaningful context for learning, which is more important than systematically controlling their occurrence. Younger students are more apt to identify alliteration they hear before they can read. (They may be taught visual recognition of the same letter beginning multiple words in a sentence, but this does not develop phonemic awareness, which develops and/or can be taught even earlier.)

30. D: Teachers should use a broad variety of instructional materials to support student vocabulary development, including not only literature and expository texts (A) but also newspapers, magazines (B), trade books, content-specific texts, technology (C), and other sources of vocabulary words to provide students with the richest and most authentic array of contexts possible for the greatest quantity and quality of exposure to and learning of vocabulary.

31. A: Multiple research studies have found that teaching phonological awareness skills to kindergarteners with delayed language development has enhanced their language development. Researchers also recommend involving speech-language pathologists (SLPs) and their instructional methods as effective in teaching phonological awareness skills (B). Phonological awareness involves being able to recognize and change phonemes (speech sounds) without any reference to meanings (C) of words, syllables, or morphological units. Researchers and others instructing kindergarteners in phonological awareness skills have provided training at both the individual phoneme level (identifying and differentiating phonemes, matching initial and final phonemes, deleting phonemes, blending phonemes, etc.) and above (D) the phoneme level (syllable, word, and rhyme awareness).

32. D: *Assonance* is the term used to describe repeated vowel sounds in nearby words. Assonance is often found in poetry and can be used to affect mood. Onomatopoeia refers to the use of sound words. Alliteration occurs when several words near one another in a text begin with the same sound. Consonance is a term used to describe repeated consonant sounds in nearby words.

33. B: This prompt focuses not only on reading fluency skills, but also on the issue of the young reader's confidence. It is very common for students who feel unsuccessful at reading to avoid the skill altogether. The teacher in this question realizes something important: it is vital to build a student's confidence with reading as he or she builds skill. In choice A there is a faulty assumption that a student could ever memorize enough words to eliminate the need to decode. While some students with processing disorders or different learning styles do rely more heavily on sight words, this practice should not be solely relied upon. In choice C the students will likely feel negatively about being asked to read young children's books; their lack of confidence may be reinforced by this plan. In choice D students may also be frustrated by the extra work they are required to do without any evidence of success with this practice. In choice B, students can build their fluency skills by creating words with various sounds, which is often easier for students than decoding as they are learning to read. As their knowledge of letter-sound relationships grows, they will become better at decoding words they see on the page. Allowing students to encode will also provide them with more chances to feel successful as they learn.

34. D: Word roots, prefixes, and suffixes are all morphological units, i.e., the smallest structural or grammatical units of words that carry meaning (e.g., the *–s* ending added to regular nouns changes them from singular to plural in number, and the *–ed* ending added to regular verbs changes them from present to past tense). Identifying morphological word parts gives students structural cues to determine word meaning. Alphabetic principle knowledge (A) is the knowledge that letters correspond to speech sounds. Combining vowel sounds (B) enables word decoding by using alphabetic principle knowledge and phonics to connect combinations of vowel letters with their combined sounds. Semantic and syntactic context (C) enables decoding unknown words by considering the meaning of the semantic context (surrounding phrase, sentence, paragraph, etc.) and the surrounding syntactic context (sentence structure and word order).

35. B: The word *first* shows that this sentence describes the beginning of Maria's family's process for planning holiday celebrations. This is an appropriate detail to follow Maria's introductory sentence. Choices A and C are not clearly relevant to the topic sentence. While these may be important details later, neither of these sentences should follow the topic sentence. Choice D should be included later in the composition, as the word *afterwards* shows that the described step occurs later.

36. A: Characters. Children enjoy identifying with a character and experiencing life from that character's point of view. If readers do not bond with a character, they will not enjoy the story.

37. B: Many authors find story events can help readers understand both event causality and character motivation (A), as well as some of life's meaning (D). They describe story events as mental experiments that enable readers to explore (B) different meanings and ways of living. They say story events do NOT necessarily identify one specific or definitive meaning in life or prescribe one way of living for readers (C), but can define some meaning, shape, and direction in otherwise seemingly random events.

38. D: Epigrams are composed of one to a few lines of poetry designed to be memorable because of their cleverness, word choice, and brevity. An example is Benjamin Franklin's "Early to bed and early to rise/Makes a man healthy, wealthy, and wise." Odes (A), very popular during the Romantic period, are typically complex and can be lengthy. Epics (B) are long poems telling of adventures and heroic accomplishments. In English language poetry, elegies (C) are poems that lament a death or other sad event.

39. A: First graders love to listen to chapter books, but most first graders are not quite able to read chapter books on their own. The undersea fictional adventures in this book will impart a great deal of marine information while simultaneously capturing students' attention with the story. The *Whale Watchers Guide* is not a good choice since the class is not planning a whale watching trip. *Moby Dick* is a well-known adult book, which first graders would not understand. *The Pacific Ocean* will probably offer a lot of marine information, but may not capture first graders' interests.

40. B: Main characters are usually dynamic, meaning they change throughout the story. Generally, these changes result from one or more conflicts in the story and how the character responds to them. Choice A is incorrect because static characters are characters who are not developed throughout the story, whereas dynamic characters are well-developed. Choice C is incorrect because round characters are ones that have complex and changeable traits. A character who does not go through any development in a story is a static character. Choice D is incorrect because authors use foils to make a main character's traits more obvious, not less obvious.

41. B: Mood refers to the emotions evoked in the reader by the literary work, whereas tone refers to the emotions or attitude of the author toward the subject matter or audience, making choice B correct. Choice C is the reverse of this, so it is not correct. Choice A is incorrect because mood and tone do not mean the same thing. Though mood and tone have different meanings, neither one is associated with particular techniques; the same literary techniques could be used for either purpose, so choice D is incorrect.

42. B: Authors of informational texts may occasionally explicitly state their point of view, but there are more cases where the author is acting as an expert, a neutral observer, or some other ostensibly objective voice. Therefore, readers will often need to infer the author's point of view. Choice A is incorrect because there is no requirement in informational writing that the author's point of view be part of the main idea. Choice C is incorrect because seeing the author's point of view is generally easier when the author is extreme or opinionated and harder when they seem neutral or balanced. This also means that some analysis is usually required, but the need for analysis does not indicate that the writing is poor, so choice D is incorrect.

43. D: Five stages identified in children's writing development are: Scribbling and drawing (A), wherein they hold crayons/pencils in their fists and explore line, space, and form; Letter-like forms and shapes (D), wherein they understand that written forms symbolize meanings and begin drawing circles, squares, and other shapes, drawing figures and asking parents what they "say." In the Letters (B) stage, children can form letter shapes, usually starting with consonants, and enjoy writing their own name initials. They only gradually develop understanding of the sounds represented by the letters. In the Letters and spaces (C) stage, children develop word concepts and space correctly between words. The fifth stage is Conventional writing and spelling, including correct punctuation and purposeful writing.

44. C: In the process writing approach, elements include having students write for authentic audiences (A), interact with other students throughout the writing process (B), take personal responsibility for their written work (C), and self-evaluate their writing (D).

45. C: According to experts, research shows that teachers should explicitly teach their students writing strategies, including prewriting planning, composition, revision, and editing, by first modeling the strategies; then guiding students in practicing them; and then, once they have learned the strategies, letting students practice using them independently. They should not skip the guided practice step (A); students need assistance learning to apply demonstrated strategies before practicing on their own. Students learn better with, not without, teacher models (B), which must be presented before, not after, guided practice (D).

46. C: Writing instruction strategies proven effective by multiple research studies include brainstorming to plan before writing; explicit instruction of students by teachers in techniques for planning, revising, and editing compositions; explicit instruction in steps to follow for writing argumentation; collaborative work among students to plan, write, edit, and revise their writing in groups; and teacher modeling of writing strategies. Of these, teacher modeling should be introduced initially and then gradually faded as students gain experience and confidence with practice until they independently apply the strategies consistently.

47. A: In the organization stage of writing, the writer determines the purpose, thesis, and supporting details of the written work. In other words, the organization stage is the part of the writing process where the writer decides on the structure of the proposed written work. In this stage, the writer organizes the ideas already decided upon in the prewriting stage.

48. B: When writing dialogue, reproducing real-life conversations word-for-word could make for a boring conversation and one that does not contribute much to the story or characters. Generally, stories are best served by dialogue that is edited to omit anything boring or irrelevant. Choice A is incorrect because dialogue can be used effectively to give exposition in a less direct way. This can cause readers to engage with the story more by, for example, making inferences. Choice C is incorrect because dialect can help readers identify stock characters and can help make characters more realistic. Dialect is generally achieved with changes to standard spelling and grammar. Choice D is incorrect because generally dialogue should serve the story and should not merely punctuate exposition.

49. D: Students should not decide whether another student's essay is good writing or poor writing. Peer editing should consist of suggestions for improvement and never involve judgmental decisions about quality.

50. B: Choice B is correct because dialogue can be used to bring themes and meanings into clearer focus and change the course of the plot. Choice A is incorrect because dialogue can be used to advance the plot and to develop characters. Choice C is incorrect because dialogue should not be used merely to break up exposition, and it does not by itself slow the pace of the story. Choice D is incorrect because dialogue can be used to reproduce real-life speech patterns and to add drama to a story.

Social Science

51. B: In order to prosper, a nation should not try to increase its imports. Mercantilism is an economic theory including the idea that prosperity comes from a positive balance of international trade. For any one nation to prosper, that nation should increase its exports but decrease its imports. Exporting more to other countries while importing less from them will give a country a positive trade balance. This theory assumes that money and wealth are identical assets of a nation. In addition, this theory also assumes that the volume of global trade is an unchangeable quantity. Mercantilism dictates that a nation's government should apply a policy of economic protectionism by stimulating more exports and suppressing imports. Some ways to accomplish this task have included granting subsidies for exports and imposing tariffs on imports. Mercantilism can be regarded as essentially the opposite of the free trade policies that have been encouraged in more recent years.

52. A: The input and output data demonstrate the law of diminishing marginal returns, which states that as inputs are added during production, there eventually comes a time when increased inputs coincide with a decrease in marginal return.

53. A: GDP (Gross Domestic Product) is restricted to value produced within borders, whereas GNP (Gross National Product) is focused on value produced by companies regardless of borders.

54. D: While all social science is concerned to some extent with how societies make use of whatever resources are available to them, the production and distribution of goods is of primary concern to the economist.

55. B: Any expenditure that will increase a firm's future productivity is considered investment. Of the items listed, only the construction of a new plant matches the definition.

56. A: One example of the multiplier effect of large cities would be if the presence of specialized equipment for an industry attracted even more business. Large cities tend to grow even larger for a number of reasons: they have more skilled workers, they have greater concentrations of specialized equipment, and they have already-functioning markets. These factors all make it easier for a business to begin operations in a large city than elsewhere. Thus, the populations and economic productivity of large cities tend to grow quickly. Some governments have sought to mitigate this trend by clustering groups of similar industries in smaller cities.

57. A: When the prices farmers receive for their crops decline in a developing country, this typically results in increased urbanization. When crop prices decline, farmers can no longer make a living from their land. As a result, they often choose to migrate to cities in search of low-wage employment in the manufacturing or service sectors.

58. D: The hurricane decreased the supply of gasoline while demand remained constant. When demand is greater than supply, prices tend to go up.

59. C: Acid rain is an example of chemical weathering. When acidic chemicals are evaporated and fall as rain, they can have devastating effects on plant and animal life. Although human activity is the primary cause of acid rain, weathering chemicals can also get into the atmosphere through oceanic bacteria and volcanoes. The other three answer choices are examples of mechanical weathering. Frost wedging occurs when water seeps into a narrow space within a rock formation and then freezes. Because water takes up more space as ice and frost than it does in its liquid state, this process can cause structural damage to the rock. Heat expansion occurs when rapid changes in temperature cause rocks to expand, leading to cracks and fissures. Salt wedging occurs when water flowing into a rock brings salt in with it. The water evaporates, but the salt is left behind, and over time the deposits of salt can create pressure within the rock.

60. A: The Nile River flooded regularly and reliably, irrigating the crops of the ancient Egyptians. This best explains the stability of Egyptian culture. Answer (B) can be rejected because though the Nile River is expansive; its size did not prevent the Egyptian people from settling elsewhere. Answer (C) can be rejected because the Valley of the Kings, an ancient Egyptian city, did not separate Upper and Lower Egypt. Answer (D) can be rejected because, even if true, interaction with other cultures is more likely to lead to a dynamic, changing culture than a stable, unchanging culture.

61. B: The Erie Canal opened in 1825 and created a water route between the Hudson River and Lake Erie. Water routes have historically been cheaper and easier than overland ones and the Erie Canal was originally proposed in the 1700s as a means of providing a shipping route to assist in settling the areas west of the Appalachian Mountains. The Mississippi River is to the west of the Great Lakes; its source is in Minnesota and it discharges into the Gulf of Mexico approximately 100 miles downstream of New Orleans, Louisiana. The Susquehanna River runs through New York, Pennsylvania, and Maryland and is the home of Three Mile Island, the site of the United States' largest nuclear disaster. The Lehigh River is located in eastern Pennsylvania.

62. C: About 30 percent of the surface of the Earth is covered by land.

63. C: Lying at a little more than 23° south of the equator, the Tropic of Capricorn is the border between the Southern Temperate Zone to the south and the Tropical Zone to the north. The southern hemisphere is tilted toward the sun to its maximum extent each year at the winter solstice in December. The northernmost latitude at which the sun can appear directly overhead is at the Tropic of Cancer during the summer solstice. The northern and southern hemispheres are separated by the equator at 0° latitude. The eastern and western hemispheres are separated by the prime meridian at 0° longitude.

64. B: On a political map, countries are represented in different colors, and countries that share a border are not given the same color. This is so that the borders between countries will be distinct. Political maps are used to illustrate those aspects of a country that have been determined by people: the capital, the provincial and national borders, and the large cities. Political maps sometimes include major physical features like rivers and mountains, but they are not intended to display all such information. On a physical, climate, or contour map, however, the borders between nations are more incidental. Colors are used on these maps to represent physical features, areas with similar climate, etc. It is possible that colors will overrun the borders and be shared by adjacent countries.

65. A: A city located at 6,000 feet above sea level is likely to have a cooler climate, all other things being equal. Since air is less dense at higher altitudes, it holds heat less effectively, and temperatures tend to be lower as a result. Precipitation is not as strong an indicator of temperature. Some areas that receive moderate or large amounts of precipitation are cooler (temperate and continental climates), while some areas that receive lots of precipitation, like the tropics, are warmer.

66. B: Lines of longitude, which run north-south from pole to pole, are used to separate time zones. Houston, Texas, and Fargo, North Dakota, which are on almost the exact same line of longitude, are both in the Central Time Zone; however, they are not in the same state, do not have the same climate, and are not equidistant from the equator. To calculate distance from the equator, the latitude of the city would need to be known.

67. B: Congress has the authority to shape the judicial branch. The Supreme Court once operated with only six members. Nine has been the standard number since 1869.

68. A: The Supreme Court interprets the law and the Constitution. The inferior courts are bound to uphold the law as the Supreme Court interprets and rules on it.

69. B: *Marbury v. Madison* started with the election of Thomas Jefferson as third President of the United States. The lame-duck Congress responded by issuing a large number of judicial patents, which the incoming president and Secretary of State refused to deliver to their holders. Marbury, who was to receive a patent as Justice of the Peace, sued to demand delivery. What makes this case important is the decision which declared the judiciary's ability to overturn legislation that conflicted with the Constitution. The case states:

"It is emphatically the province and duty of the judicial department to say what the law is. Those who apply the rule to particular cases must, of necessity, expound and interpret that rule. If two laws conflict with each other, the courts must decide on the operation of each.

"So if a law be in opposition to the Constitution; if both the law and the constitution apply to a particular case, so that the court must either decide that case conformably to the law, disregarding the Constitution; or conformably to the Constitution, disregarding the law; the court must determine which of these conflicting rules governs the case. This is of the very essence of judicial duty.

"If, then, the courts are to regard the Constitution, and the Constitution is superior to any ordinary act of the legislature, the Constitution, and not such ordinary act, must govern the case to which they both apply."

Later, the ruling states: "The judicial power of the United States is extended to all cases arising under the Constitution." It was in this way that the Supreme Court achieved its now traditional ability to strike down laws and to act as the final arbitrator of what is and is not allowed under the US Constitution.

70. D: The vice president also serves as the president of the Senate. If a tie occurs in the Senate, the vice president casts his vote to break the tie.

71. C: There are no formal qualifications for members of the judicial branch. However, having a background in law is an informal qualification that is considered when appointing Article III judges.

72. D: Federalists who helped frame the Constitution believed the central government needed to be stronger than what was established under the Articles of Confederation. Anti-federalists were against this and feared a strong federal government. A system of checks and balances was established to prevent the central government from taking too much power.

73. B: In the Dred Scott case of 1857, the Supreme Court ruled that Dred Scott was not a citizen and had no right to bring his case to court. This set the legal precedent that enslaved people were not citizens and, therefore, could not expect legal protection from the government or the courts.

74. A: The president of the United States serves as commander-in-chief, but the writers of the Constitution, who feared how authority was used by monarchs, limited the president's power in this role. The president cannot declare war or make rules governing the military, although presidents have traditionally authorized the use of force without war being declared.

75. D: The process of overriding a presidential veto is described in Article I, Section 7 of the Constitution. It requires a two-thirds vote from both the House and the Senate.

76. C: The Populist movement arose in the US in the 1890s as a grassroots political movement started by southern and western farmers to fight banks, railroads, large corporations and other "elites." "Farmers United" sounds like it could be a correct choice, given the involvement of farmers, but it is incorrect. Choice A and D are also incorrect, although the "Social Gospel" movement was active around the same time period. Entrepreneurship was also on the rise during that time period.

77. C: Choice C is the BEST and only definition of the initiative process: It allowed citizens to introduce legislation proposals at a local or state level by gathering petitions, and proposals would then be addressed by lawmakers or placed on ballots for a vote. The other answer choices give definitions of "referendum" (A), "recall" (B), and also describe simply visiting a state legislature to give testimony about an issue (D), none of which define the "initiative" process.

78. C: While wounds from war most certainly killed more than a few, European disease laid waste to vast swaths of Native American people who had no immunity to the foreign diseases which the Europeans carried. The forced marches took place in the mid-19th century under Andrew Jackson's presidency and are thus removed from the time frame in question.

79. D: After being Cherokee deputy chief for two years, Mankiller became the Cherokee Nation's first woman principal chief in 1985. She was reelected in 1987 and 1991, serving for 10 years. She worked to improve Cherokee health care, educational, and governmental systems and was also a women's rights activist. She published books on history; state–tribal diplomacy; a traditional Cherokee cookbook; her autobiography, *Mankiller: A Chief and Her People* (1993); coauthored *Every Day Is a Good Day: Reflections by Contemporary Indigenous Women* (2004) with a foreword by her close friend feminist leader Gloria Steinem; and taught for three months in 1996 at Dartmouth College. She received many awards, including the Presidential Medal of Freedom in 1998. After her death in 2010, President Obama honored her for having "transformed the nation-to-nation relationship between the Cherokee Nation and the federal government" and inspiring women nationwide. Option A described Marie Curie. Option C describes Malala Yousafzai. Option D describes Maya Angelou.

80. B: Although Charlemagne himself may not have believed his authority was conferred by the pope, Charlemagne's successors sometimes used the title "Holy Roman Emperor" (given to them by the pope) as a basis for their authority. Thus, the title "Holy Roman Emperor" strengthened the notion that political authority was conferred by the pope. Charlemagne united much of Europe under a single ruler prior to being named Holy Roman Emperor. While Catholicism may have been the recognized religion, the naming of Charlemagne as Holy Roman Emperor did not make it so. After being so named, Charlemagne did not renounce his conquests. This eliminates options A, C, and D respectively.

81. D: Despite the growing amount of literacy in the 1500s, due principally to the invention of the printing press and the availability of texts, the majority of Europeans remained illiterate.

82. D: Choice D lists true contributions by John Jay to early America. Choice A is partly correct about the first Chief Justice, but Jay was a Minister to Spain, not to France. Choice B correctly places him in New York, but he did not sign the Declaration or become mayor of New York City. Choice C has Minister to Spain correct, but Jay did not serve in George Washington's army during the war.

83. B: Growth of industry was concentrated in urban areas, which cyclically drew laborers into cities, growing the population of cities and increasing efficiency and quality in industry.

84. B: He was calling for a return to peaceful times and a focus on domestic issues, as opposed to a focus on international war. Choice A is a good guess because the president would want a good economy, and industry had been busy during WWI before falling off slightly after the war, but the statement in choice B is a better summary of what President Harding meant.

85. D: It is not true that the Gilded Age is a term whose origins have not been identified clearly. In 1873, Mark Twain and Charles Dudley Warner co-authored a book entitled *The Gilded Age: A Tale of Today*. Twain and Warner first coined this term to describe the extravagance and excesses of America's wealthy upper class, who became richer than ever due to industrialization. Furthermore, the Gilded Age was the era of the "robber barons" such as John D. Rockefeller, Cornelius Vanderbilt, J.P. Morgan, and others. Because they accumulated enormous wealth through extremely aggressive and occasionally unethical monetary manipulations, critics dubbed them "robber barons" because they seemed to be elite lords of robbery. While these business tycoons grasped huge fortunes, some of them—such as Andrew Carnegie and Andrew Mellon—were also philanthropists, using their wealth to support and further worthy causes such as literacy, education, health care, charities, and the arts. They donated millions of dollars to fund social improvements. Carnegie himself dubbed this large philanthropic movement the "Gospel of Wealth." Another characteristic of the Gilded Age was the Beaux Arts architectural style, a neo-Renaissance style modeled after the great architectural designs of the European Renaissance. The Panic of 1893 ended the Gilded Age and began a severe four-year economic depression. The Progressive Era followed these events.

86. C: The ancient Mayan civilization was located in Central America. Today, the land of their former empire comprises Guatemala, Belize, Honduras, and El Salvador in Central America and also the Yucatan Peninsula and the south of Mexico. The ancient civilization of the Incas was located in what is now Peru in South America. The ancient civilization of the Aztecs lived in what is Mexico today.

87. A: Agriculture was not a viable economic model for New Englanders. Although the colonists were mainly from England and Scotland, few were merchants before arriving in the colonies. Slavery existed in the north, although it was less important to the economy than it was in the agricultural south. New England colonists were not actively competing with their neighbors to the immediate south.

88. A: By the 5th grade, students should have been exposed to the concept of point of view. They should understand that various individuals will possess different perspectives on the same topic or event; additionally, teachers should illustrate how the United States has evolved from the desire to embrace different points of view, generally speaking. Choice B refers to research and inquiry skills that are taught toward the beginning of the high school curriculum. Choice C is usually found in middle-school lessons. The final choice relies on the ability to understand different points of view, but is typically taught in middle-school, following the initial lessons mentioned in choice A.

89. A: The passage is a firsthand account of witnessing, via television, the first moon landing, and is best suited for teaching students what that experience was like. Although the source does briefly describe the surface of the moon, this description is not the main idea of the passage and is too brief to be well-suited for a unit on this topic. This eliminates option B. Option C can be eliminated because the author of the passage makes clear that he or she was very young at the time of the landing, and the author explicitly states that he or she is not clear how it was possible to show the moon landing live on earth. Finally, option D can be rejected because although the author does describe a change the author's family's own television, the passage makes no general claims about changes in television use.

90. B: Being a citizen involves multiple responsibilities and exercising just as many freedoms with responsibility. Citizenship rests on the assumption that the individual will behave according to social rules and in a way that is best for the society as a whole. The best way to teach young students to be citizens is to allow them to actually *be* citizens. This scenario suggests that all students have jobs that contribute to their classroom in some way: sharpening pencils, watering plants, gathering papers, and various other tasks. The students also get practice identifying important issues and voting democratically upon them to come to a decision. While they may not vote on every single issue that arises, the teacher can guide students to participate in effective ways. With this practice, students will become accustomed to helping others and contributing to their community in a positive way.

91. C: To help young children understand citizenship concepts, teachers should help them understand the purposes and functions of laws and rules. Understanding these will help them realize that our government is made up of individuals and groups who create and enforce laws. Teachers should also help young children understand that laws limit the powers of authorities (A), preventing them from abusing their roles. Teachers should explain that laws determine the responsibilities of individual citizens (B) like themselves and their family members. They should also point out to young children that laws and rules help to make life and society more predictable, secure, and orderly (D).

92. B: In order for students to understand causal relationships among historical events and processes, they must understand chronology. Analysis of historical succession patterns is a standard expected of high school students, not middle school students (A). However, students are expected to be able to interpret data from timelines by middle school, not high school (C). To instruct younger students in chronology, teachers *should* use narratives (D); e.g., histories written in story style, biographies, and historical literature. Such materials engage younger students' attention, help them to understand the historical motivations and actions of individuals and groups, and enable them to comprehend the relationships among antecedents, actions and events, and consequences as well as temporal event sequences.

93. D: Teachers can use not only history books (A); they can also assign students to read well-constructed and well-written biographies (B) of famous figures in history and works of historical literature (C), which set even fictionalized stories within real historical periods and events. Historical narratives written in "storytelling" style are also good for engaging student attention while establishing chronological sequences in history.

94. D: An inquiry-based approach to teaching social studies promotes young children's natural inclination for curiosity and exploration. Encouraging students to ask questions and make observations as they learn about the world around them establishes a foundation for understanding how major themes related to social studies apply to their daily lives and on a larger scale. Teachers can foster inquiry in the classroom by creating engaging learning opportunities that encourage students to devise their own questions and motivate them to seek the answers through active, hands-on investigation. In this situation, leading a discussion about similarities and differences between clothing from various climates leads students to question and want to learn why individuals in other parts of the world may dress the way they do, thus cultivating an inquiry-based learning experience.

95. D: A practical application of content learned involves action, not merely knowledge. Options A and C, although they describe content that students would reasonably learn in a class or unit on the structure of the US government, do not describe applications of content, or applications of a social studies education. Therefore, options A and C can both be rejected. Option B does involve action and not merely the acquisition of knowledge. However, it is not as directly tied to learning the structure of the US government as option D, informed participation in US political processes. This is because informed participation in school elections is quite possible without knowing the structure of the U.S government. Informed participation in US political processes requires knowledge of the structure of the US government (i.e., voting on an issue requires an understanding of where a given candidate stands on that issue).

Science

96. B: The Earth's environment consists of the atmosphere (the air we breathe), the hydrosphere (water), and the lithosphere (the land).

97. D: Sedimentary rock is formed on the surface of the Earth and deposited in layers as the result of natural processes like erosion. Igneous (A) rocks are formed from volcanic eruptions. Obsidian (B) is just one type of igneous rock. Metamorphic (C) rocks form deep in the Earth's crust through heavy pressure and/or heat, which metamorphose or change sedimentary and igneous rocks far below the surface.

98. C: The Sun's energy is the energy source behind Earth's weather patterns, but since the Sun's energy only directly reaches a fraction of Earth's landmass, other factors play an enormous role in distributing the energy globally. The ocean absorbs the Sun's energy and transports it throughout the world, acting as the primary driving force behind global climate and weather. Wind belts, the Earth's orbit, and atmospheric conditions also play a role in driving global weather.

99. A: Pros of wind energy include space efficiency, no pollution, and low operational costs. Cons of wind energy include wind fluctuation, threats to wildlife, and the expense to manufacture and install.

100. C: The majority of the solar energy that reaches Earth is absorbed by the oceans, which make up 71 percent of the Earth's surface. Because of water's high specific heat capacity, oceans can absorb and store large quantities of heat, thus preventing drastic increases in the overall atmospheric temperature.

101. A: The eye wall of a hurricane has the strongest winds and the greatest rainfall. The eye wall is the tower-like rim of the eye. It is from this wall that clouds extend out, which are seen from above as the classic outward spiral pattern. A hurricane front is the outermost edge of its influence; although there will be heavy winds and rain in this area, the intensity will be relatively small. The eye of a hurricane is actually a place of surprising peace. In this area, dry and cool air rushes down to the ground or sea. Once there, the air is caught up in the winds of the eye wall and is driven outward at a furious pace.

102. B: Pros of solar energy include the facts that it is renewable, abundant, environmentally friendly, low maintenance, and silent. Cons of solar energy include that it is expensive and intermittent and requires a lot of space. Solar panels require rare minerals like indium and tellurium and at this point are only about 20% efficient in harvesting energy—putting them behind several other alternative methods. Other solar harvesting methods besides the photoelectric effect include concentrated solar and water heating.

103. D: Subduction occurs at convergent boundaries. Subduction is the process that occurs when two tectonic plates collide and one plate moves under the other plate.

104. A: The average distance from the earth to the sun is equal to one astronomical unit (AU). An AU is equal to 93 million miles and is far smaller than a light-year or a parsec. A light-year is defined as the distance light can travel in a vacuum in one year, and is equal to roughly 63,241 AU. A parsec is the parallax of one arcsecond and is equal to 2.0626×10^5 astronomical units.

105. B: Unlike other organic molecules, lipids are not water soluble. They are largely nonpolar, and therefore hydrophobic. Lipids are not built from repeating monomers; this is characteristic of carbohydrates, proteins, and amino acids. Enzymes are proteins that can catalyze reactions. Lipids store more energy per gram than carbohydrates and proteins.

106. D: Respiration produces carbon dioxide and water. The net equation of respiration is the reverse of the equation for photosynthesis. Respiration is a series of reactions that consume glucose and oxygen to release energy and produce carbon dioxide and water. Oxygen and glucose are the substances that are broken down in respiration.

107. D: Reproductive habits would not be considered evidence for evolution. Usually, how a species reproduces does not support nor add to the body of evidence for the theory of evolution. Reproductive habits might exemplify how any given organism can adapt to changes in its environment as a way to survive. This does not necessarily show evolution. Fossil record is evidence for evolution as it shows evolutionary change of organisms over time. DNA sequences show that organisms that are related evolutionarily also have related gene sequences. Anatomical structures such as having an internal bony structure provide evidence of descent from a common ancestor.

108. D: An inversion mutation is represented in the sequence 1 5 4 3 2 6. An inversion error is a type of mutation where an entire sequence of DNA is reversed. In this case, 2 3 4 5 has been reversed to 5 4 3 2. Answer A, breakage, in a gene can mess up its function entirely or lead to a translocation of genetic information. Answer B, deletion, is when a section of DNA is omitted or lost. Answer C, insertion, is when an extra base pair is added to a DNA sequence. Deletions and insertions can lead to a frameshift effect where entire sequences are thrown off because one nucleotide is wrong. This could result in coding for the wrong amino acid and non-functioning proteins.

109. A: A lysosome is an organelle that is thought to be linked to the aging process and contains digestive enzymes that break down food and unneeded substances. Chromatin is the structure created by DNA and various proteins in the cell's nucleus during interphase and condenses to form chromosomes. Plastids are found in plants and algae. They often contain pigments and usually help make chemical compounds for the plant. The Golgi apparatus prepares macromolecules like proteins and lipids for transport.

110. D: The muscular system includes muscles, which allow a person's body to move. The integumentary system (A) includes organs such as the skin. While injuries to the skin can limit a person's range of movement, it does not enable movement. The digestive system (B) allows a person to eat and digest food, but does not allow a person to move. The endocrine system (C) is related to hormones, not a person's ability to move.

111. A: Long-term energy storage in animals takes the form of fat. Animals also store energy as glycogen, and plants store energy as starch, but these substances are for shorter-term use. Fats are a good storage form for chemical energy because fatty acids bond to glycerol in a condensation reaction to form fats (triglycerides). This reaction, which releases water, allows for the compacting of high-energy fatty acids in a concentrated form.

112. B: Some RNA molecules in extant organisms have enzymatic activity; for example, the formation of peptide bonds on ribosomes is catalyzed by an RNA molecule. This and other information have led scientists to believe that the most likely molecules to first demonstrate enzymatic activity were RNA molecules.

113. A: Carbohydrates are the primary source of energy for the body. Proteins and lipids also provide energy, but are not as readily digestible to use actively. The Dietary Guidelines for Americans recommend that 45-65% of food intake consist of carbohydrates. Vitamins and minerals aid in metabolism and allow for cellular repair. Fats and proteins are available for energy if the body needs them, but the primary function of fats is to support cell growth and regulation of bodily functions, while the primary function of proteins is to help repair and build muscle tissue and to regulate chemical balances in the body.

114. D: Both prokaryotes and eukaryotes interact with the extracellular environment and use membrane-bound or membrane-associated proteins to achieve this. They both use diffusion and active transport to move materials in and out of their cells. Prokaryotes have very few proteins associated with their DNA, whereas eukaryotes' DNA is richly studded with proteins. Both types of living things can have flagella, although with different structural characteristics in the two groups. The most important differences between prokaryotes and eukaryotes are the lack of a nucleus and membrane-bound organelles in prokaryotes.

115. D: Vinegar is a 5% solution of acetic acid. The pH scale ranges from 0 to 14. Substances with a pH near zero are strong acids, and substances with a pH near 14 are strong bases. Substances with a pH of 7 are neutral. Bleach is a strong base, and ammonia is a relatively weak base. Water is neutral. Since vinegar is the only acid listed, the pH of vinegar is the closest to a pH of 1.

116. C: Heat transfer can never occur from a cooler object to a warmer object. While the second law of thermodynamics implies that heat never spontaneously transfers from a cooler object to a warmer object, it is possible for heat to be transferred to a warmer object, given the proper input of work to the system. This is the principle by which a refrigerator operates. Work is done to the system to transfer heat from the objects inside the refrigerator to the air surrounding the refrigerator. All other answer choices are true.

117. C: Hydrogen bonds are a special type of dipole-dipole interaction between molecules that causes a strong attraction (negative dipole to positive dipole). This interaction gives water such a high surface tension that some small organisms, such as water striders, can move across its surface. Although water molecules are polar, they do not attract non-polar molecules, such as fats or oils. Thus, choice A is incorrect. Solid water is less dense than liquid water, which is why ice floats in water and why choice B is incorrect. Choice D is incorrect because water is generally a very good solvent, especially for substances whose molecules have polar or ionic bonds. Choice E is incorrect because water cannot produce more of either H^+ or OH^-, since both would be made in equal amounts from H_2O, making it a terrible buffer.

118. B: Electrons, protons, and neutrons are subatomic particles. Electrons have the smallest mass. Protons and neutrons, which are nearly equal in mass, are several orders of magnitude more massive than electrons. Quarks are believed to be the components of protons and neutrons; while a quark has less mass than a complete proton or neutron, it still has more mass than an electron.

119. C: Predictions of the solubility of each chemical at 150 degrees Celsius can be made by extending the lines or curves. Since the data for KBr is relatively linear, it is reasonable to assume that the solubility may increase to about 130 g per 100 g H_2O. If the curves for $NaClO_3$ and KNO_3 continue along the same lines, then these predictions are too low. The prediction for NaCl is too high.

120. B: The weight of the art is $200 \text{ kg} \times 9.8 \text{ m/s}^2 = 1{,}960 \text{ N}$. This is the total force pulling DOWN on the wires. However, the tension acts along a 40° angle, and the vertical force is $T \sin\theta$. Additionally, there are two ends to the wire, which splits the tension, meaning the weight is spread across $2T\sin\theta$. So $2T\sin\theta = w$. Therefore, $T = \frac{1}{2} \times \frac{1{,}960 \text{ N}}{\sin(40°)} = 1{,}525 \text{ N}$. Note: There's also a horizontal component to the tension forces, each expressed as $T\cos\theta$. The net force of the left and right tensions is zero. Answer A is calculated using the $\cos(40°)$ instead of $\sin(40°)$.

121. C: Percent error is calculated by the following equation.

$$\text{Percent error} = \frac{\text{Experimental value} - \text{Theoretical value}}{\text{Theoretical value}} \times 100\%$$

$$\text{Percent error} = \frac{0.410 - 0.385}{0.385} \times 100\% = 6.49\%$$

The percent error for the students' specific heat of copper is 6.49%.

122. A: The period of a simple pendulum depends on the length and the rate of acceleration due to gravity. The period is independent of amplitude (to a good approximation) for amplitudes less than about 15 degrees. The period of a pendulum is unaffected by increasing the mass.

123. D: In a homogeneous solution, the substance that is dissolved is the solute. A mixture of sugar and water is a homogenous solution in which the sugar is the solute, and the water is the solvent. A mixture of salt and water is a homogeneous solution in which the salt is the solute, and the water is the solvent. A mixture of ash in air is a description of smoke, which is a colloid. A mixture of salt and pepper is a heterogeneous mixture.

124. A: If diluted, acetic acid may be disposed of by sink or sewer. Vinegar is a 5% acetic acid solution and is commonly used in the kitchen. In general, alkanoic acids with 5 or fewer carbon atoms, such as acetic acid, butyric acid, and formic acid, may be disposed of by sink or sewer. Chemicals such as benzene, acetone, and mercury should never be disposed of by sink or sewer.

125. D: For EC teachers to help children learn through scientific inquiry and discovery, one basic principle is to teach what they know, by using learning materials they find most familiar. For example, a teacher who enjoys plants can give children bean-planting activities to witness the growth process and learn about observation, measurement, comparison, etc., and also include the "Jack and the Beanstalk" story, integrating literacy with science. Additional principles include these: EC teachers should use learning materials from the everyday environment (A), like pinecones, leaves, feathers, rocks, etc. These cost nothing, are familiar to children, and they will encounter them again outside classrooms, enhancing learning. EC teachers should not only encourage children's observation but also observe themselves (B): young children teach adults as well as learn from them by generating novel uses of materials not occurring to adults. EC teachers should first let children play with and explore new materials before using them in structured activities (C) to understand purposes, uses, and care of materials.

126. A: When young children learn basic science concepts, an informal learning experience is defined as one wherein the child has choice and control over the activity, but at some point during the activity an adult provides some kind of intervention. When the child has complete choice and control of the activity and no adult intervenes at all (B), this is the definition of a naturalistic learning experience. If the child's activity is chosen and directed by an adult (C), or assigned to a group of children in preschool by the teacher (D), these are examples of structured learning experiences.

127. C: Eyewash stations should be capable of delivered rinsing fluid to both eyes for a minimum of 15 minutes. The stations should be located in an accessible area where a person can reach the station in no more than 10 seconds.

128. A: Dissection is not a general scientific process skill; it is a specific process that some students learn for surgically cutting open and examining parts of deceased or synthesized organisms. Historically, preserved dead animals were used, and still are in some programs, especially for older students, e.g., in medical schools. But more humane, extremely realistic artificial replicas and computer simulations are available today. General process skills that good EC science programs should develop include observation (B), i.e., looking at, listening to, touching, and otherwise directly examining events, things, animals, and people to learn what information is available through using one's senses and reasoning; classification (C), i.e., identifying the similarities and differences among events, things, animals, and people and grouping them accordingly; and communication (D), i.e., discussing, reporting, and hearing observations, classifications, questions, ideas, conclusions, etc., with others.

129. B: The shaking that is observed during an earthquake is a direct result of seismic waves. Seismic waves are vibrations that travel through earth when rock slippage along a fault occurs. There are two types of seismic waves: body waves and surface waves. Body waves can either be primary, or P waves, and secondary, or S waves. P waves move more quickly than S waves and create motion that radiates directly outward from the point of origin. S waves produce a shearing, or side-to-side, motion. The other type of seismic wave is a surface wave, which causes much of the shaking felt at Earth's surface.

130. A: When students are taught science, the information needs to be correct, contextualized, and explained.

131. C: Placing scientific concepts in a developmentally appropriate context for learning is necessary to build students' fundamental concept knowledge and promote understanding when approaching increasingly complex ideas. At the kindergarten level, teachers can expect students to be able to identify distinguishing features among various types of animals, such as a duck's webbed feet, a bird's feathers, or an elephant's trunk. As young children learn most effectively through play and exploration, placing lifelike models of animals into the science area allows them to actively engage with learning materials and observe differences in the animals' physical characteristics. By asking students to identify these distinguishing features as they play, this teacher prompts further inquiry and establishes the foundation for developing their initial understanding that animals physically adapt to survive in different habitats.

132. A: Young children build knowledge and skills in science through developmentally appropriate experiences that demonstrate the prevalence of major scientific concepts in daily life. Such experiences meet students where they are in terms of ability, and they place learning in an immediately applicable context for increased relevancy, engagement, and understanding. Placing trash items found on the school playground into a bin of water and watching as it becomes increasingly dirty illustrates the negative impact of litter on students' surrounding environment, thus establishing a foundation for grasping this concept on a larger scale.

133. A: A characteristic of a reputable scientific journal is that there is peer review of the quality of the research. The other choices may be characteristics of scientific journals, but these do not necessarily mean a journal is reputable.

134. D: Once a hypothesis has been verified and accepted, it becomes a theory. A theory is a generally accepted explanation that has been highly developed and tested. A theory can explain data and be expected to predict outcomes of tests. A fact is considered to be an objective and verifiable observation, whereas a scientific theory is a greater body of accepted knowledge, principles, or relationships that might explain a fact. A law is an explanation of events for which the outcome is always the same. A conclusion is more of an opinion and could be based on observation, evidence, fact, laws, or even beliefs.

135. A: Observation includes collecting evidence, using the five senses, and writing descriptions. Classifying includes grouping items based on similarities, differences, and interrelationships. Inferring includes explaining or interpreting collected evidence. Communication is reporting to others what has been found by experimentation.

136. C: For an experiment to be considered successful, it must yield data that others can reproduce. A reasonable hypothesis (A) may be considered part of a well-designed experiment. A well-written lab report (B) and computer-aided statistical analysis (D) may be considered part of an experiment that is reported on by individuals with expertise.

137. C: Jabir Ibn Hayyan, Antoine Lavoisier, Dmitri Mendeleev, and Marie Curie are associated with the study of chemistry. Isaac Newton, Albert Einstein, Richard Feynman, and Stephen Hawking are associated with the study of physics. Robert Hooke, Louis Pasteur, James Watson & Francis Crick, and François Jacob & Jacques Monod are associated with the study of biology. James Hutton, Charles Darwin, Georges Cuvier, and Alfred Wegener are associated with the study of geology.

138. C: The independent variable is the variable that is changed in the experiment in order to determine its effect on the dependent variable or the outcome of the experiment. The dependent variable results from the experimenter making only one change to an experiment that can be repeated with the same results. Mrs. Jones's class was comparing the effects of sugar and artificial sweetener on the overall color of cookies once they are baked; thus, the one thing that should be changed in the experiment is the sugar and artificial sweetener in the recipe. All of the other ingredients stay the same. For the experiment to be valid and not influenced by any other variables, the students should keep the temperature and baking time the same, as these could affect the color of the cookies as well.

139. B: The first step in the scientific method is to ask a research question to which we want to find an answer. The second step is to formulate a hypothesis (A), which is an educated guess about the answer to the research question. The third step is to conduct an experiment (C) to test the hypothesis. The final steps are to decide whether the results of the experiment support or fail to support the hypothesis and then to report this to others (D).

140. D: Not all scientific literature is reliable. Students must learn to distinguish between sources that are consistent with experimental evidence and those that are biased or misleading in their conclusions. Scientists study one another's work to direct and support original research, but they recognize that interpretations of data may vary and that existing theories are always subject to testing and revision.

Mathematics

141. C: Using the points $(-3,1)$ and $(1,-11)$, the slope may be written as $m = \frac{-11-1}{1-(-3)}$ or $m = -3$. Substituting the slope of –3 and the x- and y-values from the point $(-3,1)$, into the slope-intercept form of an equation gives $1 = -3(-3) + b$, which simplifies to $1 = 9 + b$. Subtracting 9 from both sides of the equation gives $b = -8$. Thus, the linear equation that includes the data in the table is $y = -3x - 8$.

142. B: There are 60 months in 5 years. Since a quarter is 3 months, the following proportion may be written.

$$\frac{250}{3} = \frac{x}{60}$$

We solve by first cross-multiplying.

$$3x = 15{,}000$$

Then, divide both sides of the equation by 3.

$$x = 5{,}000$$

Therefore, Quinn will have deposited \$5,000 into the account after 5 years.

143. A: The test point of (0,0) indicates that shading should occur above the line with the steeper slope. The same test point indicates that shading should occur below the other line. The overlapped shading occurs between these two lines, in the lower left.

144. C: When solving radical equations, check for extraneous solutions.

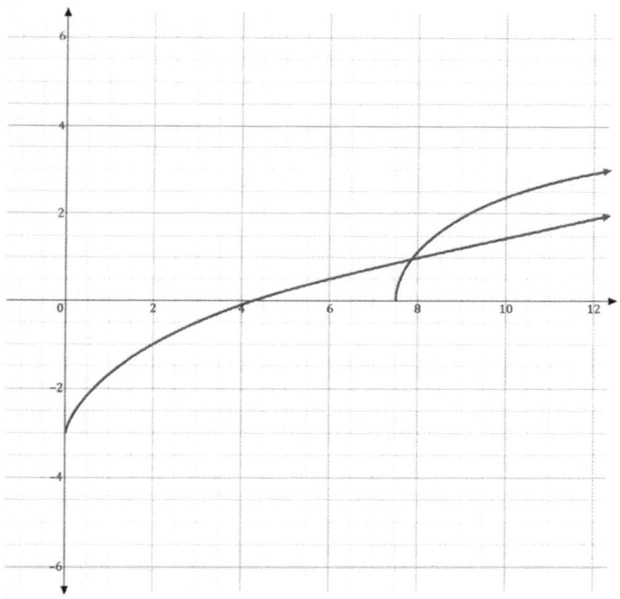

$$\sqrt{2x} - 3 = \sqrt{2x - 15}$$
$$\left(\sqrt{2x} - 3\right)^2 = \left(\sqrt{2x - 15}\right)^2$$
$$2x - 6\sqrt{2x} + 9 = 2x - 15$$
$$-6\sqrt{2x} + 9 = -15$$
$$-6\sqrt{2x} = -24$$
$$\sqrt{2x} = 4$$
$$2x = 16$$
$$x = 8$$

Check:
$$\sqrt{2(8)} - 3 = \sqrt{2(8) - 15}$$
$$\sqrt{16} - 3 = \sqrt{16 - 15}$$
$$4 - 3 = \sqrt{1}$$
$$1 = 1$$

Since the solution checks, it is a valid solution. Notice that the graphs $y = \sqrt{2x} - 3$ and $y = \sqrt{2x - 15}$ intersect, which confirms there is a solution.

145. D: Since Hannah spends at least \$16, the relation of the cost of a package of coffee to the minimum cost may be written as $4p \geq 16$. Alternatively, the inequality may be written as $16 \leq 4p$.

146. B: The surface area of a sphere may be calculated using the formula $SA = 4\pi r^2$. Substituting 7.5 for r gives $SA = 4\pi(7.5)^2$, which simplifies to $SA \approx 706.5$. So the surface area of the ball is approximately 706.5 square inches. There are twelve inches in a foot, so there are $12^2 = 144$ square inches in a square foot. In order to convert this measurement to square feet, the following proportion may be written and solved for x: $\frac{1}{144} = \frac{x}{706.5}$. So $x \approx 4.91$. It would take approximately 4.91 square feet of paint to cover the globe.

147. B: A cube has six square faces. The arrangement of these faces in a two-dimensional figure is a net of a cube if the figure can be folded to form a cube. If choice B is folded, the bottom square in the second column will overlap the fourth square in the top row, so the figure does not represent a net of a cube. The other figures represent three of the eleven possible nets of a cube.

148. A: This may be solved in a few different ways, each of which involves calculating the area of two rectangular sections whose areas can be calculated directly. The area of the "L" can be split into two pieces: a 300 ft by 50 ft section and a 50 ft by 50 ft section, or, secondarily, a 250 ft by 50 ft section and a 100 ft by 50 ft section. In either case, the areas can be calculated directly and then summed. The alternative is to view the "L" as a larger rectangle that has had a smaller rectangle removed from it. In this method, the large rectangle is a 300 ft by 100 ft section, and the smaller rectangle is a 250 ft by 50 ft section. These areas can be calculated and the smaller subtracted from the larger. In both methods, the area comes out to 17,500 square feet.

149. D: The following proportion may be written and solved for x: $\frac{24}{6} = \frac{x}{0.75}$. Use cross multiplication to solve for x.

$$24 \times 0.75 = 6x$$
$$18 = 6x$$
$$3 = x$$

Thus, the dog is 3 feet tall.

150. B: The area of a parallelogram is base × height, or $A = bh$, where b is the length of the base of the parallelogram and h is the length of an altitude to that side. In this problem, $A = 6 \text{ ft} \times 4 \text{ ft} = 24 \text{ ft}^2$. Remember, use the length of BE, not the length of CD for the height.

151. A: Kyra's monthly salary may be modeled as $\frac{1}{3}x = 1{,}050$. Multiplying both sides of the equation by 3 gives $x = 3{,}150$.

152. C: If \$70, the amount used to buy more lemons, represents 35% of Herbert's earnings, then 1% corresponds to $\frac{\$70}{35} = \$2$. To determine how much profit he takes home, multiply the dollar amount that represents 1%, which is \$2, by 15 to get $\$2 \times 15 = \$30$. Therefore, Herbert takes home \$30 in profit.

153. B: Sophia needs to find multiples of 3 (3, 6, 9, 12, 15, ...) and multiples of 4 (4, 8, 12, 16, ...) and find the least common multiple between them, which is 12. The greatest common divisor of 3 and 4 is 1. The least common divisor between two numbers is always 1. The greatest common multiple can never be determined. Therefore, the correct answer is choice B.

154. A: The first operation to be performed is multiplying five by four and three. This question requires knowledge of the order of operations, or the sequence in which arithmetic functions should be performed in a complex number sentence. The order of operations is parentheses, exponents, multiplication, addition, and subtraction. In this problem, the first step is to resolve the parenthetical expression. This can be done either by multiplying five by four and three and then multiplying the products, or by multiplying four and three and then multiplying this product by five.

155. D: The set of whole numbers is represented as $\{0, 1, 2, 3, \dots\}$. The set of counting numbers is represented as $\{1, 2, 3, \dots\}$. Thus, the set of whole numbers includes all counting numbers plus zero, so the set of counting numbers is a subset of the set of whole numbers.

156. C: A number that is divisible by 6 is divisible by 2 and 3. A number is divisible by 2 if it is even, and it is divisible by 3 if the sum of the digits is divisible by 3. For example, the number 12 is divisible by 2 and 3, so it is also divisible by 6.

157. A: Exponents, like square roots and powers of numbers, come before addition, subtraction, multiplication, and division in the mathematical order of operations. Calculations inside of parentheses are done before those outside of them, not vice versa. Multiplication and division are done before addition and subtraction, not vice versa. Multiplication and division have the same rank in the order, and addition and subtraction have the same rank. With operations having the same rank, the rule is to go from left to right in the calculation. (A mnemonic for this order is PEMDAS, i.e., Parentheses, Exponents, Multiplication and Division, Addition and Subtraction. Various phrases have been invented as acrostics for these initials, e.g., "Please Excuse My Dear Aunt Sally.")

158. C: The number 589 can be estimated to be 600. The number 9 can be estimated to be 10. The number of chicken nuggets is approximately 600×10, which is 6,000 nuggets. Therefore, the correct choice is (C).

159. C: Olivia's paycheck x may be modeled by $\frac{1}{4}x = 120$. Multiplying both sides of the equation by 4 gives $x = 480$. Her paycheck is $480.

160. C: The set of integers is represented as $\{\ldots -3, -2, -1, 0, 1, 2, 3, \ldots\}$. The set of rational numbers includes all of these as well as any number that can be represented as a fraction of two integers, where the denominator is not zero. So the set of integers is a subset of the set of rational numbers.

161. C: The number of times Olivia can expect to roll a 4 is equal to the product of the theoretical probability of getting a 4 for one roll, $\frac{1}{6}$, and the number of rolls, 10. Thus, Olivia can expect to roll a 4 $\frac{1}{6} \times 10$ times, or $\frac{5}{3}$ times. Even though Olivia cannot realistically roll a 4 $\frac{5}{3}$ times, this is theoretically how many times she would roll a 4 with 10 die rolls.

162. D: Two z-scores should be calculated, one for each student's score. The first z-score may be written as $z = \frac{68-80}{8}$, which simplifies to $z = -1.5$. The second z-score may be written as $z = \frac{84-80}{8}$, which simplifies to $z = 0.5$. The percentage of students scoring between these two scores is equal to the sum of the two mean-to-z areas. A z-score with an absolute value of 1.5 shows a mean-to-z area of 0.4332. A z-score of 0.5 shows a mean-to-z area of 0.1915. The sum of these two areas is 0.6247, or 62.47%.

163. C: The mean value is calculated as the sum of the values (175) divided by the number of values (7). Thus, the mean is 25. The standard deviation, s, of the sum of the squared differences between each value and the sample mean is 48. Substituting 7 for n gives $n - 1 = 6$. Dividing 48 by 6 yields 8. Taking the square root of 8 yields a sample standard deviation of approximately 2.8.

164. B: The probability of non-mutually exclusive events A and B occurring may be written as $P(A \text{ or } B) = P(A) + P(B) - P(A \text{ and } B)$. There are 3 even numbers on the die, so the probability of rolling an even number is $\frac{3}{6}$. There are 2 numbers greater than 4, so this probability is $\frac{2}{6}$. There is 1 number, 6, that is both even and greater than 4, so this probability is $\frac{1}{6}$. Thus, $P(A \text{ or } B) = \frac{3}{6} + \frac{2}{6} - \frac{1}{6} = \frac{4}{6} = \frac{2}{3}$.

165. C: To find the average, add together all the numbers and then divide by how many there are (in this case three). In order to add decimal numbers, write them one above the other with the decimal points aligned and carry out the addition normally, placing the decimal point in the same position in the result:

$$\begin{array}{r} 2.02 \\ 0.275 \\ +\ 1.98 \\ \hline 4.275 \end{array}$$

Now, to divide, just carry out the division normally but put the decimal point in the same position in the quotient as it appears in the dividend:

$$\begin{array}{l} 1.425 \\ 3\overline{)\,4.275} \\ \underline{3} \\ 1\,2 \\ \underline{1\,2} \\ 07 \\ \underline{6} \\ 15 \\ \underline{15} \\ 0 \end{array}$$

166. D: To be able to make accurate estimates of quantities, children must first understand relative and comparative concepts, such as bigger than, smaller than, more of, less of, etc. The process of estimating numbers and amounts in lieu of actual exact measurements helps young children to *learn* math vocabulary words (A) like *around, about, more than, less than,* etc., rather than vice versa. By practicing estimation, children also learn how to make predictions appropriately (B) and attain reasonable estimates (C), rather than the other way around.

167. D: Adding zero. Adding zero does not assist students in understanding subtraction. Physically taking some objects away from an array of objects, working a problem with a missing addend like $7 + \_\_ = 13$ helps students learn that $13 - 7 = 6$. Moving to the left on a number line is another way of helping students understand subtraction.

168. B: Measurement is not only a formal system for quantifying amounts and numbers that specify sizes, times, weights, etc. (A). It is also used informally in everyday life. As such, it is a valuable skill that young children can use to recognize and find relationships among real-world objects, outside of academic exercises. Young children are not restricted to standardized rulers, scales, clocks, calendars, etc. (C). They also practice measuring things using whatever is available, e.g., comparing objects to the length of their fingers, hands, feet, etc., or to pieces of string; comparing the heft of an object to that of a block or other toy for weight; comparing how long someone is gone to the duration of a TV show, etc. Measuring practice *does* help children learn to compare object sizes/weights and time periods (D).

169. C: Printed mathematical formulas are an example of abstract mathematical concepts presented abstractly. Young children cannot access such concepts in abstract presentations. However, they can learn to understand abstract concepts when they are presented using concrete manipulatives like tangrams for shape recognition (A), or for reproducing and designing patterns, solving spatial problems, etc.; large, magnetized numbers and number boards (B) for doing math computations concretely; play money and toy cash registers (D) for monetary numerical activities; linking cubes, color tiles; and many other math manipulatives, which are available for teachers/schools to purchase, and/or which teachers can create in homemade versions using commonly found objects.

170. B: Problem solving. Because an item is missing in the middle of the pattern, the process asked for cannot be counting or addition. Solving this puzzle does not involve manipulation of objects.

171. A: Young children need concrete objects to manipulate to learn geometry concepts. In early childhood, they think concretely and thus need to see, touch, and manipulate real things to help them understand abstract concepts; therefore, their memorizing theorems (B) at this age, when most children cannot even read let alone understand them, would be ineffective. Children should be given everyday life activities that teach geometric concepts—e.g., cutting their sandwiches into different geometric shapes, naming these for them, and letting them assemble and/or rearrange the pieces—*before* rather than after (C) they learn formal geometry basics, as activities that are part of daily life are relevant to young children and an effective way to teach concepts. Instructions to draw geometric diagrams (D) are more appropriate when children are older and have learned geometry concepts from interacting with solid objects and also have better-developed fine motor skills. Certainly, adults can help them draw shapes, but this should not be a first and/or isolated exercise.

172. A: Choice (A) is correct because standards for fourth grade state that students will be able to use a protractor to determine the approximate measures of angles in degrees to the nearest whole number. Choices (B), (C), and (D) are stated in the standards for fifth grade.

173. A: When children engage in problem-solving activities, they develop skill with regulating their own thinking, feelings, and behaviors. These are critical to their development into mature individuals and members of society. Problem-solving also encourages children to be flexible, not rigid (B) as they consider alternate methods and solutions and experiment with them. Good problem-solving skills do not necessarily result in quick action (C). Problem-solving activity does not promote dangerous risk-taking (D); however, it does promote their willingness to take reasonable risks.

174. A: Since area is two dimensional, the units for area have an exponent of 2, such as in^2, yd^2, cm^2, or m^2. Choice B includes a unit of length (yd) and a unit of volume (yd^3). Choice C includes only units of length. Choice C includes a square unit of time (s^2). Therefore, the correct choice is A.

175. D: While individual students will progress mathematically at varying rates, it is important that teachers are aware of the general expectations for typical skill development associated with each grade level. This is necessary for teachers to identify areas of individual student need so that they can differentiate and incorporate appropriate supports into instruction as well as recognize the signs of a developmental delay or learning disability. By third grade, students should have acquired a degree of fluency in adding and subtracting whole numbers within 100. If a student is continuously struggling to do so despite the implementation of academic supports, it may indicate a learning disability or delay and would require further evaluation to determine the need for special education services.